What Is the Gospel, and How to Share It

What Is the Gospel, and How to Share It

Todd M. Fink

What Is the Gospel, and How to Share It

Understand the Essence of the Gospel and How to Share It Effectively

by

Todd M. Fink

Published by Selah Book Press

Cover Illustration Copyright © 2020 by Selah Book Press

Cover design by Selah Book Press

Copyright © 2020 by Todd M. Fink

ISBN-13: 978-1-944601-46-1

First Edition

All rights reserved. No part of this publication may be reproduced or transmitted in any form or by any means, electronic or mechanical, including photocopy, recording, or any information storage retrieval system, without permission in writing from the copyright owner.

Scripture quotations are taken from the New American Standard Bible®,
Copyright © 1960, 1962, 1963, 1968, 1971, 1972, 1973, 1975, 1977, 1995 by The Lockman Foundation
Used by permission. (www.Lockman.org)

The Holy Bible, English Standard Version® (ESV®)
Copyright © 2001 by Crossway,
a publishing ministry of Good News Publishers.
All rights reserved.
ESV Text Edition: 2007

The Holy Bible, New International Version®, NIV® Copyright © 1973, 1978, 1984, 2011 by Biblica, Inc.® Used by permission. All rights reserved worldwide.

The Holy Bible, New King James Version®. Copyright © 1982 by Thomas Nelson, Inc. All rights reserved.

The NET Bible®, New English Translation (NET) Scripture quoted by permission. Quotations designated (NET) are from the NET Bible® copyright ©1996-2006 by Biblical Studies Press, L.L.C.

Unless otherwise noted, Scripture quotations are from the NASB version of the Bible.

Scripture in bold is emphasis added by the author.

ABBREVIATIONS

NASB	New American Standard Bible
ESV	English Standard Version
NIV	New International Version
NKJV	New King James Version
NET	New English Translation

Table of Contents

Introduction 1

Chapter 1: The Gospel Is Under Attack 3

Chapter 2: What Is the Gospel? General Foundation 10

Chapter 3: What Is the Gospel? Bad News Part 1 15

Chapter 4: What Is the Gospel? Bad News Part 2 26

Chapter 5: What Is the Gospel? Good News 50

Chapter 6: What Must We Believe to Be Saved? 62

Chapter 7: What Is Saving Faith? 76

Chapter 8: How to Share the Gospel in Seven Clear Steps ... 98

Chapter 9: What to Do After Salvation 108

Chapter 10: Seven Ways God Speaks to the Unsaved 127

Chapter 11: Four Main Excuses Used Against the Gospel . 153

Chapter 12: How to Start & Converse About the Gospel.... 170

Chapter 13: What Attitudes to Have in Sharing the Gospel 180

Chapter 14: What God Does When We Share the Gospel .. 191

Chapter 15: Are You a Fisherman? 199

Chapter 16: Success & Failure in Sharing the Gospel......... 208

Bibliography 217

About the Author 219

Other Books by Todd M. Fink 220

Connect with Todd (Mike) 221

Introduction

Many Christians today have a laid-back approach to the gospel. Most don't share it that much, and many don't really even understand what it is.

Moreover, the gospel being preached from many pulpits today is concerning. It's often unclear, incomplete, and inaccurate. For something so dear to the heart of Christ, and that for which He died on the Cross, it's unfortunate we don't share the same passion as Christ for its clarity. If we truly want to be like Jesus, then it's paramount we understand the gospel and know how to share it. That's the goal and purpose of this book.

My deepest longing in writing about the essence of the gospel and how to share it is to be 100% biblical. I simply want to let God speak through His word about it, and not add or take away from what He says in any way. While oftentimes we might feel uncomfortable or find it difficult to understand what God says in Scripture, our job is to discover through careful and responsible analysis of His word what He's saying, and then believe and obey it.

Therefore, this book will contain much Scripture. Rather than just referencing the verses, they are included in the book so you can read and ponder them. Please take the time to prayerfully contemplate these verses and not skip over them, even if you know them already. God's word is living and fresh. Each time we read it, and especially if our context is different, God reveals new insights and truths.

The greatest act of love is to expound and teach the truth accurately. On the contrary, the greatest lack of love is to alter and neglect aspects of the truth because they might seem culturally insensitive or difficult. This is especially true when it comes to the gospel. If we don't get it right, then salvation and eternity rest in the balance.

Christ said some very sobering and fearful words: *"Not everyone who says to Me, 'Lord, Lord,' will enter the kingdom of heaven, but he who does the will of My Father who is in heaven will enter. 22 Many will say to Me on that day, 'Lord, Lord, did we not prophesy in Your name, and in Your name cast out demons, and in Your name perform many miracles?' 23 And then I will declare to them, '**I never knew you; depart from Me**, you who practice lawlessness'"* (Matt. 7:21-23).

It's very possible many might not be in heaven because they believed in an incomplete or false gospel. Therefore, the greatest lack of love would be to share an unbiblical gospel. For this reason, let's strive together to understand what the gospel is, and how to share it biblically and effectively.

Chapter 1

The Gospel Is Under Attack

What Is the Gospel and How to Share It

The Gospel Is Under Attack

Soon after the gospel was first preached, attacks from the Jews, non-believers, Satan, and worldly forces began assaulting its essence. Nothing has changed over the past 2,000 years. The gospel always has been and always will be under attack. Why? Because it's the vehicle through which we are saved. If Satan can twist and distort the gospel, then he can effectively wage war on the salvation of countless souls and their eternal destiny.

Therefore, we find many warnings in the New Testament about the need to understand the gospel, protect its clarity, defend it, contend for it, and share it accurately.

The Gospel Is Under Attack by Those Outside and Inside the Church

When the Apostle Paul was saying his goodbyes to the elders of the church in Ephesus, he warned them to be on their guard and to take heed because there would be those who would try to distort the truth of the gospel and God's word:

Acts 20:28–31: *Be on guard for yourselves and for all the flock, among which the Holy Spirit has made you overseers, to shepherd the church of God which He purchased with His own blood. 29 I know that after my departure **savage wolves will come in among you, not sparing the flock**; 30 and **from among your own selves***

Chapter 1: The Gospel Is Under Attack

*men will arise, speaking perverse things, to draw away the disciples after them. 31 Therefore **be on the alert**, remembering that night and day for a period of three years I did not cease to admonish each one with tears.*

Paul declared that after his departure, some would intentionally go in among the church and try to draw Christ's followers away from the truth. Paul also says that there would even be some from inside the church fellowship that would try to do the same. It's the same today, and if we're attentive and awake, we'll realize it's still happening.

Therefore, God warns us to be alert, take heed, be watchful, and protect our churches and the gospel from these attacks.

The Gospel Is Under Attack by Satan and His Demonic Realm

Not only is the gospel under attack by those outside and inside the church, but also by Satan and his demonic host:

2 Corinthians 11:13–15: *For such men are false apostles, deceitful workers, disguising themselves as apostles of Christ. 14 No wonder, for even **Satan disguises himself as an angel of light**. 15 Therefore it is not surprising if **his servants also disguise themselves as servants of righteousness**, whose end will be according to their deeds.*

We can often be slumberous and passive to what Satan is doing and believe that anyone who preaches or shares the gospel is doing it clearly and correctly. We must also take into account that even well-intentioned people who share the gospel can be used by Satan to communicate a partial or distorted version of it.

Additionally, God says that as we approach the latter days before His return, there will be a heightened attack by Satan, and many will depart from the faith due to demonic influence and doctrines:

1 Timothy 4:1: *Now the Spirit expressly says that in latter times some will depart from the faith, giving heed to* ***deceiving spirits and doctrines of demons****.*

Many of those who fall away may do so because they believed and followed a watered-down or false version of the gospel.

There Is Only One True Version of the Gospel, and Any Alteration Transforms It into a False Gospel

God is so concerned about the essence and clarity of the gospel that He says any variation from the true version is a different gospel. He also warns that anyone who teaches and alters the true version of the gospel is to be cursed:

Galatians 1:6–9: *I am amazed that you are so quickly deserting Him who called you by the grace of Christ,* ***for a***

Chapter 1: The Gospel Is Under Attack

***different gospel**; 7 which is really not another; only there are some who are disturbing you and want to **distort the gospel** of Christ. 8 But even if we, or an angel from heaven, should preach to you a gospel contrary to what we have preached to you, **he is to be accursed**! 9 As we have said before, so I say again now, if any man is preaching to you a gospel contrary to what you received, **he is to be accursed**!*

The Greek word for *accursed* in this passage is one of the strongest forms possible, so we can see how seriously God takes the gospel. He also repeats the word *accursed* two times, revealing that He is dead serious about the gospel's clarity.

The State of the Gospel Today

God fully knew that His most cherished truth would be attacked on all sides and, therefore, gives us many warnings about the need to understand and preserve this critical truth. Today, more than ever, the gospel is under attack and has been distorted and modified by some, even well-meaning evangelical churches and believers.

It's my observation that many Christians and churches today are only preaching part of the gospel. We do a good job of focusing on the love of God and how He wants to help us with our problems, but do a poor job of focusing on root problems like sin, a broken relationship with God, the need for a new heart and nature, and the consequences for rejecting

Christ.

For many Christians and churches today, salvation consists primarily of being saved from the difficulties of our present life, our problems, wrong choices, bad habits, and so forth. It focuses on the here and now and how we can have a happy, fulfilled, successful existence in this life. And again, it tends to neglect root issues like our sinfulness, separation from God, rejecting the lordship of Christ, and the reality of hell as a consequence for rejecting Christ.

Many messages and talks become nothing more than glorified self-help sessions that are uplifting, motivational, and positive. And the Bible is often neglected or modified to fit what we want it to say rather than letting it say what it says.

When we neglect or omit the foundational and root problems outlined in the gospel, then we are in danger of distorting the gospel, and the question becomes, "Salvation from what?"

We Need to Contend for the Faith

Preserving the essence and clarity of the gospel requires effort and work. It's a battle that really never ends. Each generation faces the challenge of allowing Satan, false prophets, and well-intentioned people, contaminate the gospel and diminish its power. Jude, inspired by the Holy Spirit, speaks about the effort

Chapter 1: The Gospel Is Under Attack

and zeal we should display in contending for the faith:

Jude 1:3–4: *Beloved, while I was making every effort to write you about our common **salvation**, I felt the necessity to write to you appealing that you **contend earnestly for the faith** which was once for all handed down to the saints. 4 For certain persons have crept in unnoticed, those who were long beforehand marked out for this condemnation, ungodly persons who turn the grace of our God into licentiousness and deny our only Master and Lord, Jesus Christ.*

What does *contend earnestly* mean? It means to fight for, pursue carefully, battle for, seek earnestly, and give it all we have. So, how are we doing in this task? Unfortunately, it appears not so well. For many churches and Christians today, their attitude is starkly different than God's command to *"contend earnestly for the faith."*

Conclusion

The gospel is under attack by both those outside and inside the church, and by Satan and his demonic realm as well. As a result, God gives us the command to contend earnestly for the faith, protect its clarity, and understand how to share it correctly and effectively. Why is this so important? Because there are eternal consequences for not doing so!

Chapter 2

What Is the Gospel?
General Foundation

Chapter 2: What Is the Gospel: General Foundation

What Does the Word "Gospel" Mean?

The term *gospel* proceeds from the Greek and means *good news*. It doesn't refer to just any kind of good news, though, but the kind that is powerful through salvation to change lives in the here and now, and the eternal destiny of those who respond to it.

The Gospel Is God's Only Way to Save Sinful Humanity

Since God is the Creator and sovereign One over His universe, He determines how people will become right with Him and saved. We don't get to choose salvation based on our terms and what our human logic deems best. After all, we are not gods who are privileged to decide how God Almighty should do things. Consider carefully what God says about how we are saved:

Acts 4:8-12: *Then Peter, filled with the Holy Spirit, said to them, "Rulers and elders of the people, 9 if we are on trial today for a benefit done to a sick man, as to how this man has been made well, 10 let it be known to all of you and to all the people of Israel, that by the name of **Jesus Christ the Nazarene, whom you crucified, whom God raised from the dead** — by this name this man stands here before you in good health. 11 He is the stone which was rejected by you, the builders, but which became the chief corner stone. 12 **And there is salvation in no one else; for there is no other name under heaven that has been given among men by which we must be saved.**"*

God certainly makes it clear that there is no other name under heaven, or within His entire universe, whereby we can be saved. It's only in Jesus Christ and His work on the Cross that salvation is found.

Christ, who was God in the flesh, and who stated that all authority in heaven and earth had been given to Him, stated:

John 14:6: *I am the way, and the truth, and the life;* ***no one comes to the Father but through Me.***

Jesus makes it crystal clear that He is the only way to God and heaven. And because He was God in the flesh, He has all the right and authority to dictate the terms of salvation:

1 John 5:11–12: *And the testimony is this, that God has given us eternal life, and this life is in His Son. 12* ***He who has the Son has the life; he who does not have the Son of God does not have the life.***

Salvation is only found in Christ. He is the only way, and no other way exists. Anyone who says otherwise is not speaking the truth.

The Foundation of the Gospel: God Is Our Creator and Loves Everyone

First, we must understand that we are all created by God, and as a result, He loves us more than we can understand or comprehend:

Genesis 1:26–27: *Then God said, "Let Us make man in*

Chapter 2: What Is the Gospel: General Foundation

Our image, according to Our likeness; and let them rule over the fish of the sea and over the birds of the sky and over the cattle and over all the earth, and over every creeping thing that creeps on the earth." 27 **God created man in His own image, in the image of God He created him; male and female He created them.**

Regardless of what we have done or who we are, we were created by God and He loves us with an everlasting love:

Jeremiah 31:3: *The Lord appeared to him from afar, saying, "***I have loved you with an everlasting love；** *therefore,* **I have drawn you with lovingkindness.**"

The love of God is a foundational aspect of who God is and how he feels about every person. He loves everyone, and deeply desires that they would be saved and spend eternity with Him in heaven:

2 Peter 3:9: *The Lord is not slack concerning His promise, as some count slackness, but is longsuffering toward us,* **not willing that any should perish but that all should come to repentance.**

John 3:16: *For* **God so loved the world,** *that He gave His only begotten Son, that* **whoever believes** *in Him shall not perish, but have eternal life. 17 For God did not send the Son into the world to judge the world, but that the world* **might be saved** *through Him.*

Romans 5:8: *But God demonstrates* **His own love toward us,** *in that while we were yet sinners,* **Christ died**

for us.

1 Timothy 2:3-4: *This is good and acceptable in the sight of God our Savior, 4 **who desires all men to be saved** and to **come to the knowledge of the truth**.*

In these verses, we come to understand that God is our Creator and loves us. He created everyone to have a relationship with Him and know Him. That's the purpose for the existence of each person.

How tragic it would be for us who are parents to have children who rejected us, didn't want to have a relationship with us, ignored us, and lived their lives as if we didn't exist. This is exactly how God feels when we ignore and refuse to have a relationship with Him.

Conclusion

Regardless of how we might feel, or view God because of what we think He has done wrong in our lives or the world, He loves each person with a deep eternal love that is beyond measure. His love is so deep that He came to earth, suffered immensely, and died on the Cross to have a relationship with us.

God's love for everyone is imperative to understand and communicate in sharing the gospel. We want people to know that God loves them, and they were created to have a relationship with Him. This is the foundation of the gospel, and that upon which the other parts of the gospel rest.

Chapter 3

What Is the Gospel?

Bad News ~ Part One

We Are All Sinful and Separated from God, Our Creator

Now while the general foundation of the gospel is that God loves us, and is our starting point in sharing the gospel, the remainder of the gospel actually begins with bad news. The bad news is that we are sinful and, therefore, separated from God and a relationship with Him:

Isaiah 59:2: *But your iniquities have made a **separation between you and your God**, and your sins have hidden his face from you so that he does not hear.*

The Role of the Book of Romans in Understanding the Gospel

To understand the gospel and share it accurately, we must understand the first six chapters of the book of Romans. This book provides one of the clearest and most in-depth presentations of the gospel. In chapters 1–3, we see the reality and depth of the bad news.

Romans Chapter 1

The bad news begins in chapter 1, and reveals that God has made Himself and His wrath against sin known to every person, so we are without excuse:

Romans 1:18–20: *For the **wrath of God** is revealed from heaven against all ungodliness and unrighteousness of men who suppress the truth in unrighteousness, 19 because that which is known about God is evident within them; for*

Chapter 3: What Is the Gospel: Bad News ~ Part One

God made it evident to them*. 20 For since the creation of the world His invisible attributes, His eternal power and divine nature, have been clearly seen, being understood through what has been made,* ***so that they are without excuse****.*

God has made known His wrath and revealed Himself to each person, so they are without excuse. Interestingly, according to God, there are no atheists. Some might claim to be, but in the depths of their heart they know there is a God because God, Himself, has revealed Himself to them.

This verse also reveals that those who reject God suppress the truth He reveals to them. Suppress means to put down, lower, hide, reject, and cover up.

As a result of suppressing the truth God has revealed, He allows a person to fall deeper into sin, which results in having a depraved mindset, or backward way of thinking:

Romans 1:28-32: *And just as they did not* ***see fit to acknowledge God any longer, God gave them over to a depraved mind****, to do those things which are not proper, 29 being filled with all unrighteousness, wickedness, greed, evil; full of envy, murder, strife, deceit, malice; they are gossips, 30 slanderers, haters of God, insolent, arrogant, boastful, inventors of evil, disobedient to parents, 31 without understanding, untrustworthy, unloving, unmerciful; 32* ***and although they know the ordinance of God****, that those who practice such things* ***are worthy of death****, they* not only do the same, but also **give hearty approval** to those who practice them.

For those who continue to reject the light and revelation God has revealed to them, God gives them over to a depraved mind. And even though they know what they are doing makes them worthy of death, they continue in it and give hearty approval to others who do the same. This reveals the intense depth of their sin.

Romans Chapter 2

God has written His laws in every person's heart and given them a conscience that convicts and reveals right and wrong to them. As a result, every person knows they have done wrong and are sinful:

Romans 2:14–15: *For when Gentiles who do not have the Law do instinctively the things of the Law, these, not having the Law, are a law to themselves, 15 in that they* ***show the work of the Law written in their hearts,*** *their conscience bearing witness and their thoughts alternately accusing or else defending them.*

Romans Chapter 3

This chapter blares out with a resounding, clashing cymbal that every person has sinned and stands guilty before God:

Romans 3:9–20: *For we have already charged that both Jews and Greeks are all under sin; 10 as it is written, "****There is none righteous, not even one****; 11 There is none who*

Chapter 3: What Is the Gospel: Bad News ~ Part One

*understands, There is none who seeks for God; 12 All have turned aside, together they have become useless; There is none who does good, There is not even one." 13 "Their throat is an open grave, With their tongues they keep deceiving," "The poison of asps is under their lips"; 14 "Whose mouth is full of cursing and bitterness"; 15 "Their feet are swift to shed blood, 16 Destruction and misery are in their paths, 17 And the path of peace they have not known." 18 "There is no fear of God before their eyes." 19 Now we know that whatever the Law says, it speaks to those who are under the Law, so that **every mouth may be closed and all the world may become accountable to God**; 20 because by the works of the Law no flesh will be justified in His sight; for through the Law comes the knowledge of sin.*

A Mounting Case that All Are Sinful

God continues to build the case that all have sinned, so there is no mistake about our condition as sinners before a holy and just God:

Romans 3:23: *For **all have sinned** and fall short of the glory of God.*

Romans 5:8: *Therefore, just as through one man sin entered into the world, and death through sin, and so death spread to all men, **because all sinned**.*

1 John 1:8-9: *If we say that **we have no sin, we are deceiving ourselves and the truth is not in us**. If we confess our sins, He is faithful and righteous to forgive us our sins and to cleanse us from all unrighteousness.*

There should be no doubt by now that God holds everyone guilty of sin. Notice, it's not how we feel about ourselves; it's what God says about us that matters. We are in no position to be judge and jury regarding our status before God. He is the judge, and it only matters what He thinks and says, and He says we are all sinners and in need of a Savior.

What Is the Definition of Sin?

How would you describe sin? What is it, and how did it first start? S. Michael Houdmann provides a brief overview of sin, what it is, and when it started:

"Sin is described in the Bible as transgression of the law of God (1 John 3:4) and rebellion against God (Deut. 9:7; Josh. 1:18). Sin had its beginning with Lucifer, probably the most beautiful and powerful of the angels. Not content with his position, he desired to be higher than God, and that was his downfall, the beginning of sin (Isaiah 14:12-15). Renamed Satan, he brought sin to the human race in the Garden of Eden, where he tempted Adam and Eve with the same enticement, 'you shall be like God.' Genesis 3 describes Adam and Eve's rebellion against God and against His command. Since that time, sin has been passed down through all the generations of mankind and we, Adam's descendants, have inherited sin from him. Romans 5:12 tells us that through Adam sin entered the world, and so death was passed on to all men because

Chapter 3: What Is the Gospel: Bad News ~ Part One

'the wages of sin is death' (Rom. 6:23)."[1]

In summary, sin is making ourselves the lord of our lives instead of God. It's establishing ourselves on the throne of our lives and making ourselves the highest authority. It's rebellion against God and ignoring Him as Lord. It's transgressing and disobeying God's laws of right and wrong, and following our own sinful ways instead. It's not having a relationship with God, loving and serving Him, but instead, loving and serving our own interests, plans, and dreams.

What About Evil, Where Did It Originate, and How Did It Come into Existence?

This question has been the topic of endless discussion and debate. It's a deep question and one that affects the nature of God. Some believe God created evil and is its author. Others believe evil originated with Satan, was passed on to Adam and Eve, and then to all mankind.

What do you believe about evil? Did God create it? From where did it come, and what is it?

Here's my brief and humble answer to these monumental questions: *Evil is a reality that exists as the result of any rational being who possesses a free will that*

---

[1] Gotquestions.org, www.gotquestions.org/definition-sin.html, accessed 01/17/2020

chooses wrong instead of good. God did not necessarily create evil; it's just a reality or byproduct that exists as a result of any rational being who is endowed with a free will.

When God decided to create the angels and humans, He had a decision to make. Would He create them as puppets, void of the power of choice, or would He endow them with a free will as He possesses? I believe God created us all with a real, genuine free will. When a rational created being is endowed with choice, then the ability to choose evil is an option. The only way to eliminate this would be to eliminate free will.

This free will does not affect God's sovereignty in any way or form. God knows the beginning from the end and takes into account all our decisions in His master plan for creation.

God created Satan and all the angels perfect, but many used their free will and rebelled against God. God created Adam and Eve perfect, but they used their free will and chose evil as well. I believe God knew they would all sin but did not make them sin, nor is He the author of their sin. Therefore, evil is using our free will to sin instead of obeying God.

What Is the Worst Sin that Exists?

Are all sins equal? If not, are some sins worse than others? It's true that all sin is sin, and that the tiniest sin is enough to make us guilty and keep us from heaven. However, not all sins are equal. This becomes clear as

Chapter 3: What Is the Gospel: Bad News ~ Part One

we look at how God punished different sins in the Old Testament. Some sins required the offender to die by stoning; other sins just required the guilty person to repay what was stolen or damaged. Therefore, not all sins are equal. Murder is worse than stealing, and adultery is worse than lying. Once again, this is seen by the judgments rendered in each case

With this being said, what is the worst sin anyone could commit? Is it murder, adultery, or something else? Contrary to what most would answer, the worst sin is not having a relationship with God and loving Him with all our being:

Matthew 22:34–40: *But when the Pharisees heard that Jesus had silenced the Sadducees, they gathered themselves together. 35 One of them, a lawyer, asked Him a question, testing Him, 36 "Teacher, which is the great commandment in the Law?" 37 And He said to him,* **"You shall love the Lord your God with all your heart, and with all your soul, and with all your mind."** *38* **This is the great and foremost commandment.** *39 The second is like it, "You shall love your neighbor as yourself." 40 On these two commandments depend the whole Law and the Prophets.*

So, if the greatest commandment is to love God with all our being, then the worst sin is not doing so.

This is vitally important to understand. The greatest sin of any person is to reject God and not love Him. It's not murder, adultery, stealing, lying, and so forth.

These are all sins, but they don't compare to the severity of rejecting a relationship with God and not loving Him.

When sharing the gospel, this truth should be emphasized. Many times, good people can honestly say that they haven't murdered, committed adultery, stolen, and so forth. But this is not their greatest sin. Their greatest sin is not having a relationship with God and loving Him.

Conclusion

After sharing the foundation of the gospel, which is that God loves us, the rest of the gospel begins with bad news. We must understand this point clearly, or the good news (the gospel) loses its power and effect. So, to the degree we neglect and skip over the bad news, will be the degree the good news loses its purpose for which God intended. In fact, if there is no bad news, then there is no good news!

This is one of the great weaknesses in the church and among Christians today. We generally focus on the good news and gloss over or entirely neglect the bad news. This causes a partial and incomplete gospel to be shared. As a result, salvation may not be obtained, and instead, a person might just add Jesus on to their life to fix them up a bit, alleviate some problems, and help them live a more successful, peaceful, and trouble-free life.

Chapter 3: What Is the Gospel: Bad News ~ Part One

Studies show that when the bad news of the gospel is neglected or omitted, the rate of those who fall away from Christ skyrockets upward. Why is this so? Well, maybe it's because people only see Christ as an accessory, not as Lord. They fail to see and understand the root problems of their sinful and rebellious hearts. Their mindset remains selfish, only wanting blessings and happiness from God, and discarding what they don't like about His commands. They are unwilling to make Christ the Lord of their lives, and instead, remain the lord of their lives living as they please.

In summary, we have lost our relationship with God, our Creator, and as a result, have a sinful heart. Therefore, we have no desire to please God and are selfish and sinful. We trample underfoot God's laws of right and wrong and choose our own sinful laws instead.

Again, our greatest sin is rejecting a relationship with God and not loving Him as our Father and Creator. If the greatest command is to love the Lord our God with all our heart, soul, mind, and strength, then our greatest sin is not doing so.

Chapter 4

What Is the Gospel?

Bad News ~ Part Two

Chapter 4: What Is the Gospel? Bad News Part ~ Two

The Cost of Being a Sinner and Rejecting God's Offer of Salvation Through Jesus Christ

The bad news continues in this part of the gospel. The first aspect of the bad news is that we are all guilty of sin as charged by God and are sinful and separated from Him. We don't have a relationship with God through Jesus Christ and are lost in our sins. We are the lords of our lives instead of God.

The second part of the bad news deals with the consequences of our sinfulness. I must warn you, though, this is the most difficult for both Christians and non-Christians to believe and process, as it's excruciatingly severe and sobering. In fact, it's beyond our ability to fully grasp.

Why is this part of the gospel so difficult to share and talk about? Because it deals with the existence of hell and whether or not it's eternal.

The Sinfulness of Every Person

Sin infected the human race in the Garden of Eden shortly after creation:

Genesis 2:15-17: *Then the Lord God took the man and put him into the garden of Eden to cultivate it and keep it. 16 The Lord God commanded the man, saying, "From any tree of the garden you may eat freely; 17 but from the tree of the knowledge of good and evil you shall not eat, for in the day that you eat from it **you will surely die."***

When God talks about death in relation to sin, it normally refers to both spiritual death in the present and eternal death or separation from God in hell in the future.

Genesis 3:1-7: *Now the serpent was more crafty than any beast of the field which the Lord God had made. And he said to the woman, "Indeed, has God said, You shall not eat from any tree of the garden?" 2 The woman said to the serpent, "From the fruit of the trees of the garden we may eat; 3 but from the fruit of the tree which is in the middle of the garden, God has said, "You shall not eat from it or touch it, or you will die." 4 The serpent said to the woman, "You surely will not die! 5 For God knows that in the day you eat from it your eyes will be opened, and you will be like God, knowing good and evil." 6 When the woman saw that the tree was good for food, and that it was a delight to the eyes, and that the tree was desirable to make one wise, **she took from its fruit and ate; and she gave also to her husband with her, and he ate**. 7 Then the eyes of both of them were opened, and they knew that they were naked; and they sewed fig leaves together and made themselves loin coverings.*

At this point in history, sin entered the human race, and both spiritual and physical death were set in motion.

Note that the first result of sin was a broken relationship with God. It says that Adam and Eve hid from God: *"They heard the sound of the Lord God walking in the garden in the cool of the day, and the man and his wife*

Chapter 4: What Is the Gospel? Bad News Part ~ Two

hid themselves from the presence of the Lord God among the trees of the garden" (Gen. 3:8).

This affirms the truth we spoke of in the previous chapter that the greatest sin is a broken relationship with God, not murder, adultery, stealing, lying, and so forth.

The Consequences of Sin

As a result of the fall of Adam and Eve in the Garden of Eden, mankind has now lost their relationship with God, and the law of physical and spiritual death has been set in motion. This now applies to every person as well. If a person is not born again and reunited with God through the work of Jesus Christ on the Cross, then eternal separation from God in hell awaits them.

Therefore, the cost or payment of sin is not only spiritual death in this life but also eternal death in hell. In simple terms, hell is separation from God, which means separation from life, love, goodness, joy, peace, relationships, purpose, hope, and so forth. When a person refuses to be reunited with their Creator through Jesus Christ, they are choosing separation from Him instead.

This separation, also known as hell, is described in part by Christ:

Mark 9:43–48: *If your hand causes you to stumble, cut it* *off; it is better for you to enter life crippled, than, having your two hands, to **go into hell**, into the **unquenchable fire**, 44 where their **worm does not die**, and the **fire is not quenched**. 45 If your foot causes you to stumble, cut it off; it is better for you to enter life lame, than, having your two feet, to be **cast into hell**, 46 where their **worm does not die**, and the **fire is not quenched**. 47 If your eye causes you to stumble, throw it out; it is better for you to enter the kingdom of God with one eye, than, having two eyes, to be **cast into hell**, 48 where their **worm does not die**, and the **fire is not quenched**. 49 For everyone will be salted with fire.*

Interestingly, it was Jesus who developed and brought to the forefront the doctrine of hell. In fact, He talked more about hell than heaven. For Christ, there is no question as to its existence. He repeatedly described it in many ways so we would not be confused:

Matthew 13:49–50: *So it will be at the end of the age; the angels will come forth and take out the wicked from among the righteous, 50 and will throw them into the **furnace of fire**; in that place there will be **weeping and gnashing of teeth**.*

Revelation 20:11–15: *Then I saw a great white throne and Him who sat upon it, from whose presence earth and heaven fled away, and no place was found for them. 12 And I saw the dead, the great and the small, standing before the throne, and books were opened; and another book was opened, which is the book of life; and the dead were judged*

Chapter 4: What Is the Gospel? Bad News Part ~ Two

*from the things which were written in the books, according to their deeds. 13 And the sea gave up the dead which were in it, and death and Hades [place of the grave] gave up the dead which were in them; and they were judged, every one of them according to their deeds. 14 Then death and Hades were thrown **into the lake of fire**. This is the **second death, the lake of fire**. 15 And if anyone's name was not found written in the book of life, he was thrown **into the lake of fire**.*

Notice that the phrase *lake of fire* is mentioned three times in this passage. Whenever God says something repeatedly, it means He wants to embed that truth deep into our hearts and minds.

Is Hell a Real Place, and Is It Eternal?

Does hell really exist, and if so, is it eternal? In all of Scripture, there's no doubt as to its existence. It's mentioned repeatedly, and Jesus spoke about it more than anyone else.

The word hell is translated from the Greek word Gehenna, which was a literal place just outside the southeastern walls of Old City Jerusalem. It was a dumping ground for the sewage and waste of the city. It consisted of crawling worms and maggots from rotting flesh of animals and food waste, and fires burned continually to destroy the garbage and impurities. Therefore, Gehenna was used as a symbol of hell. It's mentioned 12 times in the New Testament, with Jesus using it 11 times.

In addition to the example of Gehenna, many other terms are used to describe hell as well:

- It's a burning lake of fire of brimstone that never ends (Matt. 25:46; Mark 9:43-48; Rev. 20:14, 21:8).
- It's eternal destruction away from the presence of God (2 Thess. 1:9).
- It's a place of weeping and gnashing of teeth (Matt. 13:50).
- It's where Satan and the demons will suffer for all eternity (Matt. 25:41; Rev. 20:14).
- It's an eternal prison of darkness (2 Pet. 2:4).
- It's where the worm never dies (Mark 9:48).
- It's where the fire is never quenched (Mark 9:48).
- It's a burning furnace (Matt. 13:42).
- It's where everyone will be salted with fire (Mark 9:50).
- It's a place of utter darkness (Jude 1:13).

The eternal existence of hell as a real place where Satan, demons, and the unsaved will spend eternity has been the orthodox view of Christianity since the time of Christ. It's also the majority view today.

However, virtually all false religions, and even some Christians, don't believe hell exists.

There are also some who believe hell exists, and that

Chapter 4: What Is the Gospel? Bad News Part ~ Two

it's an eternal place where Satan and demons will suffer for all eternity, but that humans there will not suffer for eternity but be annihilated at some point in time. Their belief is called annihilationism. We'll look at it in more detail in the next section.

For now, we'll just look at whether hell itself is eternal or not. Consider the following verses that speak about the eternal nature of hell:

Revelation 20:10: *And the devil who deceived them was thrown into the **lake of fire** and brimstone, where the beast and the false prophet are also; and they will be **tormented day and night forever and ever.***

Not only is the devil cast into the lake of fire, but the unsaved whose names are not written in the Book of Life as well:

Revelation 21:8: *But for the cowardly and unbelieving and abominable and murderers and immoral persons and sorcerers and idolaters and all liars, their part will be in the **lake that burns with fire and brimstone**, which is the **second death**.*

Matthew 25:31-33: *But when the Son of Man comes in His glory, and all the angels with Him, then He will sit on His glorious throne. 32 All the nations will be gathered before Him; and He will separate them from one another, as the shepherd separates the sheep from the goats; 33 and He will put the sheep on His right, and the goats on the left.*

A few verses later, Christ reveals what will happen

to the goats on His left:

Matthew 25:41: *Then He will also say to those on His left, "Depart from Me, accursed ones, into the **eternal fire** which has been prepared for the devil and his angels."*

Christ then speaks about the eternal nature of each place the sheep (believers) and the goats (unsaved) will go:

Matthew 25:46: *These [the goats] will go away into **eternal punishment**, but the righteous into **eternal life**.*

Now note that the same word *eternal* is used to describe both hell and heaven (it's the same word in Greek as well).

There are some today who don't believe hell is eternal. The problem with this view is that it also makes heaven temporary or non-eternal. I don't know of any reputable scholar or theologian that believes heaven is not eternal. However, a growing number of people believe hell is not eternal. This proposes a huge problem with the doctrine of heaven and its eternal nature.

Are Humans Destroyed in Hell, or Do They Exist There Forever?

Some today acknowledge that hell exists, but that most humans who are there, if not all, will be destroyed at some point in time and cease to exist. Their belief is called annihilationism. A few evangelical

Chapter 4: What Is the Gospel? Bad News Part ~ Two

Christians hold this view, but they are in the minority.

There are also some who believe that after suffering in hell for some period of time, all humans there will be saved and go to heaven. Their belief is called universalism. Very few evangelical Christians hold this view.

In this section, we'll discuss the belief of annihilationism, as it's more common among Christians, and attempt to understand if it's true or not.

There are three main families of verses that support this view. These verses contain the words or phrases: (1) eternal destruction, (2) destroy soul and body in hell, and (3) perish.

Because this book is not a full treatise on the doctrine of hell, we'll just look at one verse from each family:

2 Thessalonians 1:9: *These will pay the penalty of **eternal destruction**, away from the presence of the Lord and from the glory of His power.*

Because this verse contains the phrase *"eternal destruction,"* some believe that the humans who are in hell will be destroyed at some point in time and cease to exist. However, the word eternal is attached to destruction, so I believe the word destruction doesn't mean annihilation but a state of eternal death and suffering.

The second verse uses the word ***destroy***, which is a form of the word destruction:

Matthew 10:28: *Do not fear those who kill the body but are unable to kill the soul; but rather fear Him who is able to **destroy both soul and body in hell**.*

Because the word ***destroy*** is used in this verse, some believe that the humans in hell will be annihilated at some point in time.

The third verse uses the word ***perish***. Therefore, it's believed, like the other preceding verses, that humans in hell will cease to exist at some point in time:

John 3:16: *For God so loved the world, that He gave His only begotten Son, that whoever believes in Him shall not **perish**, but have eternal life.*

Based on these kinds of verses, some believe in annihilationism.

Part of their belief also resides in what they call, "The Moral Argument." They reason that God is not just for punishing a person for all eternity for their short time of sin while on earth. In other words, the punishment doesn't fit the crime.

Now I must confess, the idea of someone suffering for eternity in hell seems quite severe, and my personal preference would be that those in hell would cease to exist at some point in time, but that's just my preference, not what reality is. Nonetheless, I think we

Chapter 4: What Is the Gospel? Bad News Part ~ Two

must submit our reasoning and justice into the hands of God and what Scripture says, not our own human preferences.

Now for argument's sake, let's say it's true that hell is not eternal for humans, and that at some point in time those there will be destroyed and cease to exist. Even if this were the case, they would still suffer horrifically for a period of time, and then be destroyed and miss the glory of what they could have had in heaven. This scenario is still drastic, painful, and sad.

With this being said, I still believe that if we look at the entire body of the teaching on hell, the verses that speak of it as eternal are overwhelming, so I must conclude that the words *destroy* and *perish* mean the same thing as *eternal destruction*. Therefore, I believe eternal destruction is just that, eternal. It's not destruction that results in annihilation, but a state of destruction or death described as eternal.

I also believe the words **destruction, destroy**, and **perish**, refer to a wasted life that forfeited heaven, and all its glory, in exchange for hell. Therefore, the terms speak of a lost opportunity and eternal death, not annihilationism.

As mentioned before, the same word *eternal* is used to describe both hell and heaven:

Matthew 25:46: *These will go away into **eternal punishment**, but the righteous into **eternal life**.*

For those who don't believe hell is eternal, they are forced to concede that heaven also is not eternal because the same word *eternal* is used to describe both places. This presents a major theological problem that would be classified as heresy.

Moreover, when talking about those in hell, Christ repeatedly used the phrases: "***unquenchable fire**, where their **worm does not die, and the fire is not quenched**"* (Mark 9:43-44). These phrases seem quite clear that hell does not end or that those there are destroyed at some point in time. In addition, there are many other verses that describe hell as eternal.

Interestingly, most have no problem with Satan and the demons suffering in hell for eternity, but some do for humans. However, Scripture says that the unsaved are cast into the same eternal lake of fire as Satan and the demons: *"Then He will also say to those on His left, "Depart from Me, accursed ones, into the **eternal fire which has been prepared for the devil and his angels**"* (Matt. 25:41).

Now regardless of what you believe about whether hell is eternal or not, or how long a person might suffer there before they cease to exist, I'm sure we can all agree that what Christ and the New Testament authors say about it is not positive. It would be a place I would want to avoid at all cost. It's also a place I wouldn't want to gamble my soul on regarding its existence or eternal nature. The consequences are just too great for

Chapter 4: What Is the Gospel? Bad News Part ~ Two

error!

Based on the complete body of teaching regarding the eternal nature of hell, I believe it's clear that hell is eternal, and those in hell will live there forever. It's a sober reality, but one I believe Scripture teaches.

If There Is No Hell, Then Salvation from What?

For those who don't believe in hell, then the great theological question that must be answered is: "Salvation from what?" What is it from which we are saved? Are we just saved from our problems, wrong choices, unhappiness, suffering, and so forth? Are we just saved from annihilation so that we don't cease to exist at some point in time? Or do we suffer for a bit in hell, and then we're all saved after some determined point in time when God feels we have paid the sufficient price?

For those who don't believe in hell, or its eternal nature, they have the heavy burden of answering these questions, and if answered wrong, eternal consequences hang in the balance!

If There Is No Hell, Why Did Jesus Die on the Cross?

If there is no hell, then Christ's death on the Cross is diminished, and the gospel becomes virtually irrelevant. It also would be a horrific slap to the face of Jesus as He suffered excruciatingly for our sins so we can be saved. It takes all the suffering Christ endured, both physically and spiritually, and reduces it to ashes.

For those who deny hell, they would claim that the purpose of Christ's sacrifice on the Cross was to reveal God's love and be a good example to follow. These views do contain a certain amount of truth, but I believe they drastically fall short of the true purpose for which Christ died on the Cross.

Now while the doctrine of hell seems harsh and difficult, it's not up to us to use our human logic to judge its existence. It's a doctrine that is repeatedly mentioned by Christ and the New Testament authors, so our job is to believe it, not eradicate its existence because we don't like it, or it seems too harsh for our understanding.

Many people today rightly state that we should be more like Jesus. Well, kindly said, this not only includes believing and speaking about the pleasant and positive truths of Scripture, but the difficult ones as well. However, most people and churches today are not like Jesus. They rarely or never talk about the judgments of God and the reality of hell.

Does God Send People to Hell?

Someone has said that God doesn't send anyone to hell, but they choose to go there of their own free will. Hell is simply the absence of God and all His blessings. When a person doesn't want anything to do with God,

Chapter 4: What Is the Gospel? Bad News Part ~ Two

then God allows them to go where they will be separated from Him and His blessings. The following verse clarifies how hell is separation from God:

2 Thessalonians 1:6–9: *For after all it is only just for God to repay with affliction those who afflict you, 7 and to give relief to you who are afflicted and to us as well when the Lord Jesus will be revealed from heaven with His mighty angels in flaming fire, 8 dealing out retribution to those who do not know God and to those **who do not obey the gospel of our Lord Jesus**. 9 These will pay the penalty of **eternal destruction, away from the presence of the Lord and from the glory of His power**.*

For those who don't desire a relationship with God, then hell is their only other option. They are choosing the absence of God, and hell is their place of choice. God is not willing that any should perish but that all would be saved and spend eternity with Him in heaven:

2 Peter 3:9: *The Lord is not slow about His promise, as some count slowness, but is patient toward you, **not wishing for any to perish but for all to come to repentance**.*

However, if a person rejects God and His offer of salvation, then again, separation from God in hell is their place of choosing. God does not want them to go there but grants them their desire to be separated from Him and, therefore, they are the ones choosing hell instead of God's presence in heaven.

The Fear of Judgment and the Human Heart

We get a glimpse into how God made the human heart by noting the way He uses the fear of judgment in dealing with mankind.

When the children of Israel entered the Promised Land, they gathered at Shechem to renew their covenant with the Lord (Deut. 27, 28). Half of the tribes of Israel stood on Mt. Gerizim to pronounce blessings for obedience to God's commands (Deut. 28:1-14), and the other half stood on Mt. Ebal to pronounce curses for disobedience to God's commands (Deut. 28:15-68).

The tribe of Levi had a separate role in that they pronounced pure curses for disobedience, with no mention of any blessings (Deut. 27:9-26).

In total, God spoke 65 verses (83%) that dealt with curses for disobedience and 14 verses (17%) that dealt with blessings for obedience. Additionally, another account of blessings and cursings for the nation of Israel is found in Leviticus 26, and shows the same general percentages. This significant difference between blessings and cursings should cause reflection. Why would God be so imbalanced in the attention given to the curses over the blessings? He also followed this same pattern throughout the Old Testament.

We see a similar pattern in the life of Christ as well.

Chapter 4: What Is the Gospel? Bad News Part ~ Two

He spoke overwhelmingly more about hell than heaven, and the judgments of God were a continual theme in His preaching. In fact, Christ is the leading voice on the subject of hell and spoke of it more than any other New Testament figure.

What do the themes of curses and blessings found in Leviticus and Deuteronomy, and the strong focus on judgment and hell in Christ's preaching, teach us about the human heart? It seems to indicate that the human heart is created in such a way by God that it responds better to the fear of judgment than the reward of blessings. It doesn't mean that blessings don't have an impact, as God did refer to them often, but judgment sobers the heart up and causes it to take notice.

Speaking About the Judgments of God

God made us and knows we respond better to judgment than blessings. We can take or leave blessings, but we can't take or leave judgment for disobedience. In other words, blessings are optional, but judgment is not.

If we don't speak of the judgments of God in sharing the gospel, people may only choose to obey God if they think His blessings are worth the effort. If they don't think they are worth it, they'll "pass" on them as they'll have no fear of judgment for doing so. In other words, if judgment is removed from the table, and blessings are the only option from which to choose, then people will just decide whether the blessings are worth it or not. If they decide the blessings aren't worth it, then in their minds, they'll have nothing to lose but the blessings as there will be no consequences otherwise.

However, when judgment is brought into the equation and put on the table, then people are faced with the realization that their misbehavior will incur God's judgment. For example, a child might choose to take or leave a reward for good behavior, but they can't choose whether or not they will be disciplined for bad behavior.

By clearly communicating the reality of the judgments of God, both the unsaved and saved will be faced with certain consequences: (1) For the nonbeliever, they'll have to decide whether or not they want to pay the eternal price of suffering in hell for rejecting Christ. (2) For the believer who lives in sin and refuses to repent, they'll have to decide whether or not disobedience to God is worth incurring His discipline in their lives, the loss of fellowship with Him, and the loss of eternal rewards.

Because it seems clear that the human heart responds better to judgment than blessings, it's imperative that we include the judgments of God in communicating Scripture and the gospel to others.

Chapter 4: What Is the Gospel? Bad News Part ~ Two

The Cost of Hiding the Judgments of God

The avoidance of the judgments of God affect the message of salvation. Today, in an attempt to eliminate negativity from the church atmosphere, many evangelistic salvation calls soften or pass over the sinfulness of mankind, the consequences of sin, judgment, and hell. They primarily focus on the love of God and His blessings. This is also the tendency among individuals who share their faith as well.

A gospel that omits the sinfulness of mankind and the judgments of God is incomplete. It fails to clarify the reality of coming judgment and the consequences of sin. It's like hiding the truth from a cancer patient that they are sick and will die without treatment.

Hiding the truth about judgment presents a gospel that views the judgment of God as non-existent or not that important. It's a gospel very different from that which Christ and the apostles preached. In fact, it's a false gospel.

Consequences for Neglecting the Judgments of God

If the theme of judgment and hell is neglected in sharing the gospel, then there can be severe consequences. Also, if there's an unbalanced focus on the love and grace of God, and little on the judgment and justice of God, then we can cause great deceit and destruction in the lives of many.

If we lead non-Christians to believe that there are basically no consequences for rejecting God, then we will have participated in the greatest deception of all time, and our omission of the truth may result in their eternal damnation.

I believe that if we leave out the hard truths of Scripture, we'll answer to God for doing so:

James 3:1: *Not many of you should become teachers, my brothers, for you know that **we who teach will be judged with greater strictness**.*

If we leave out the sinfulness of mankind and the judgment of hell, then we can promote a false gospel that encourages non-believers to continue in their sin, and as a result, may send them to hell. The neglect of the judgment of God can lead others to believe that it doesn't really matter how they live their lives because God's love and grace will remove all the consequences for their disobedience to Him. To promote this mentality is not love, but deception.

The Fear of the Lord Applied to the Non-Believer

For the non-believer, there ought to be an expectant horror, terror, trembling, and dread before God for the judgment and wrath that awaits them. The reality of spending eternity in hell should shake them to their core. It should shake us as well.

For those who trample underfoot the sacrifice of

Chapter 4: What Is the Gospel? Bad News Part ~ Two

Christ, and turn their back on Him and His salvation, they should shudder and tremble before God Almighty:

Hebrews 10:26–31: *For if we go on sinning deliberately after receiving the knowledge of the truth, there no longer remains a sacrifice for sins, but a **fearful expectation of judgment**, and a **fury of fire that will consume the adversaries**. Anyone who has set aside the Law of Moses dies without mercy on the evidence of two or three witnesses. How much **worse punishment**, do you think, will be deserved by the one who has trampled underfoot the Son of God, and has profaned the blood of the covenant by which he was sanctified, and has outraged the Spirit of grace? For we know him who said, "Vengeance is mine; I will repay." And again, "The Lord will judge his people."* **It is a fearful thing to fall into the hands of the living God.**

Therefore, for the non-believer who rejects Christ's offer of salvation, there ought to be an expectant horror, terror, trembling, and dread before God for the judgment and wrath that awaits them.

However, if we hide this truth from the unsaved, we are deceiving them and possibly leading them into eternal damnation. Our responsibility is to shed light on the truth so the unsaved can see the reality of what awaits them, not hide it from them.

How the Judgment of God Is Viewed Today

Many Christians and churches today have a strong focus on the love of God and a weak or practically non-existent focus on the judgments of God. Just ask yourself if you've recently heard an entire message devoted to the topic of hell or the judgments of God? Then ask yourself if you've recently heard a message about the love of God?

If you're like most, the messages you've heard about the love of God versus the messages about the judgments of God and hell are extremely disproportional. Our focus today is on the love and grace of God. The judgments of God are unpopular and viewed negatively, while love and grace are viewed as far more appealing and positive. For this reason, many neglect or omit the judgments of God.

Once again, when analyzing Christ's message in the Gospels, we see that He talked far more about the judgments of God and hell than about heaven. He did just the opposite of what most do today.

Now to clarify, God is love, and His love is an overarching truth of Scripture, but God is also a just God and will punish those who reject His love. To only focus on His love and omit His justice is not a balanced treatment of Scripture:

Numbers 14:18: *The Lord is slow to anger and abounding in steadfast love, forgiving iniquity and*

Chapter 4: What Is the Gospel? Bad News Part ~ Two

transgression, **but he will by no means clear the guilty,** *visiting the iniquity of the fathers on the children, to the third and the fourth generation.*

Conclusion

The price for rejecting a relationship with God through Jesus Christ is sobering. God loves each person more than we can understand and has done everything possible to save us. However, for those who reject Christ's offer of salvation, they are choosing to be separated from Him, not only in this life but for all eternity in hell.

From what we've seen in this chapter about the consequences of sin and the reality of hell, it becomes clear that there is indeed a place called hell for those who reject a relationship with their Creator, rebel against Him, and choose to be their own gods. For those who reject the gospel and tread underfoot the sacrifice of Christ, they will be cast into hell and suffer eternal conscious torment for all eternity.

I fully recognize the reality of hell is severe and deeply sobering. However, my desire is to be honest with Scripture and let God say what He intends to say, not change Scripture, so it fits what my human logic and feelings deem best.

Lastly, if we want to be like Jesus, we should speak about the judgments of God when sharing the gospel.

Chapter 5

What Is the Gospel?
The Good News

Chapter 5: What Is the Gospel: The Good News

The Good News Shines Bright

God loves us so much He came to earth in Jesus Christ, died on the Cross and suffered for our sins. There is no greater expression of love than this.

However, the good news will only shine bright if we have clearly communicated the bad news. If we neglect to share the bad news, then the good news is diminished and devalued. In other words, to the degree we make known the bad news will be the degree to which the good news will shine brightly. If we neglect or omit the bad news, then the good news will plummet in value. This cannot be overemphasized.

We must speak about the love of God as foundational in sharing the gospel, but again, we must include the judgment of God for those who reject His love and offer of Salvation.

The Good News Entails Forgiveness of Sin and Its Consequences

The foundational concept of the good news is that Christ has fully paid the price of our sin through His death, burial, and resurrection. Therefore, we can stand right before God, not based on our own human efforts, but based on what Christ has done for us on the Cross.

No longer do we have to live with guilt and shame because, in Christ, we have forgiveness and peace with God:

What Is the Gospel and How to Share It

1 Corinthians 15:1–5: *Now I make known to you, brethren,* **the gospel which I preached to you,** *which also you received, in which also you stand, 2 by which also you are saved, if you hold fast the word which I preached to you, unless you believed in vain. 3 For I delivered to you as of first importance what I also received, that* **Christ died for our sins** *according to the Scriptures, 4 and that* **He was buried,** *and that* **He was raised** *on the third day according to the Scriptures, 5 and that He appeared to Cephas [Peter], then to the twelve.*

In the Old Testament, we find one of the clearest passages about what Christ suffered and endured in order to pay the penalty for our sins:

Isaiah 53:4–6: *Surely our griefs* **He Himself bore,** *and* **our sorrows He carried;** *yet we ourselves esteemed Him stricken, smitten of God, and afflicted. 5 But He was* **pierced through for our transgressions,** *He was* **crushed for our iniquities;** *the* **chastening for our well-being fell upon Him,** *and by* **His scourging we are healed.** *6 All of us like sheep have gone astray, each of us has turned to his own way; but the Lord has caused the* **iniquity of us all to fall on Him.**

In the New Testament, we see numerous verses that speak of Christ's sacrifice for our sins on the Cross. We find that through the disobedience and transgression of Adam and Eve, sin came to all humanity. However, through the obedience of Christ's life and death on the Cross, salvation comes to all:

Chapter 5: What Is the Gospel: The Good News

Romans 5:18–19: *So then as through one transgression [Adam and Eve's] there resulted condemnation to all men, even so through one act of righteousness [Jesus Christ] there resulted **justification of life to all men**. 19 For as through the one man's disobedience [Adam] the many were made sinners, even so through the obedience of the One [Jesus] the **many will be made righteous**.*

Romans 5:6–9: *For while we were still helpless, at the right time **Christ died for the ungodly**. 7 For one will hardly die for a righteous man; though perhaps for the good man someone would dare even to die. 8 But God demonstrates His own **love toward us**, in that while we were yet sinners, **Christ died for us**. 9 Much more then, having now been **justified by His blood**, we shall be saved from the wrath of God through Him.*

The price of sin and rejection of God brings death, not only in this life, but eternal death as well. However, the free gift of God is eternal life in Jesus Christ. This is certainly good news:

Romans 6:23: *For the wages of sin is death, but the free gift of God is **eternal life in Christ Jesus our Lord**.*

In Christ, there is now no condemnation whatsoever for those who are in Christ Jesus:

Romans 8:1–4: *Therefore, there is now **no condemnation for those who are in Christ Jesus**. 2 For the law of the Spirit of life in Christ Jesus has set you free from the law of sin and of death. 3 For what the Law could* *not do, weak as it was through the flesh, God did: sending His own Son in the likeness of sinful flesh and as an **offering for sin**, He condemned sin in the flesh, 4 so that the requirement of the Law might be fulfilled in us, who do not walk according to the flesh but according to the Spirit.*

In summary, the good news entails forgiveness of sin, guilt, and shame through the sacrifice of Jesus Christ on the Cross. Our sins are completely forgiven and removed. This means all the sins we have committed and will ever commit. They are all paid for by Christ and separated from us as far as the east is from the west. This is certainly good news!

Psalm 103:12: *As far as the **east is from the west**, so far has **He removed our transgressions from us**.*

The Good News Entails Eternal Life

Not only are we forgiven of our sins and have the removal of guilt and shame in our lives, but we also receive eternal life. Life that will never end, life in paradise with a perfect God, with perfect people, in a perfect environment, with a perfect mind, perfect emotions, and a perfect new eternal body that will never get tired, never grow old, and will never get sick. It will be eternal bliss forever and ever. Wow! That's good news!

Romans 6:23: *For the wages of sin is death, but the free gift of God is **eternal life** in Christ Jesus our Lord.*

Chapter 5: What Is the Gospel: The Good News

John 3:16-17: *For **God so loved the world**, that He gave His only begotten Son, that whoever believes in Him shall not perish, but have **eternal life**. 17 For God did not send the Son into the world to judge the world, but that the world might be saved through Him.*

The Good News Entails Paradise Restored

Through the good news of what Jesus Christ has done for us on the Cross, that which was lost in the Garden of Eden can now be restored. Adam and Eve's relationship with God that was once intimate and personal can now be restored to us through Jesus Christ.

We can now have communion and relationship with the living God. He comes to live within us and becomes our Father, Helper, Encourager, Sustainer, and Provider. God takes care of us, watches over us, leads us, directs our steps, sustains us, loves us, and blesses us with all spiritual blessings in the heavenly places:

Ephesians 1:3-8: *Blessed be the God and Father of our Lord Jesus Christ, who has **blessed us with every spiritual blessing in the heavenly places in Christ**, 4 just as He chose us in Him before the foundation of the world, that we would be holy and blameless before Him. In love 5 He predestined us to **adoption as sons** through Jesus Christ to Himself, according to the kind intention of His will, 6 to the praise of the glory of His grace, which He freely bestowed on* *us in the Beloved. 7 In Him we have **redemption** through His blood, the **forgiveness of our trespasses**, according to the **riches of His grace** 8 which He lavished on us.*

The Good News Entails Being Born Again

Those who receive Christ as their Lord and Savior are called "Born Again" in the Bible. They become a new person with new desires, purposes, plans, and a relationship with God.

Christ said that unless a person is born again, they cannot enter the Kingdom of Heaven: *"Jesus answered and said to him, 'Truly, truly, I say to you, unless one is **born again** he cannot see the kingdom of God'"* (John 3:3).

What hope this should be for unbelievers. I believe we often overlook the reality that the unsaved are empty, dry, without purpose, meaning, lost, and guilty. We should emphasize the good news of what being born again entails. It not only saves us for eternity in heaven, but fulfills the purpose and plans of God for us in this life as well. Being born again means we are new people, we're different, brand new, a new creation of God, and filled with new purpose and direction.

The Good News Entails Being a New Creature

Well-meaning folks will often say that Christians are not perfect, just forgiven. Or, Christians are sinners like the unsaved, but just forgiven. Let me say that the saved are far more than just forgiven. We are a new

Chapter 5: What Is the Gospel: The Good News

creation in Christ, and we have a new nature and a new heart:

1 Corinthians 5:17–18: *Therefore, if anyone is in Christ, he is a **new creature**; the old things passed away; behold, **new things have come**. 18 Now all these things are from God, who reconciled us to Himself through Christ and gave us the ministry of reconciliation.*

Colossians 3:9–12: *Do not lie to one another, since you **laid aside the old self** with its evil practices, 10 and have put on the **new self** who is being renewed to a true knowledge according to the image of the One who created him 11 a renewal in which there is no distinction between Greek and Jew, circumcised and uncircumcised, barbarian, Scythian, slave and freeman, but Christ is all, and in all.*

Romans 6:4: *We were buried therefore with him by baptism into death, in order that, just as Christ was raised from the dead by the glory of the Father, we too might walk in **newness of life**.*

Those who are born again become new creatures. They are different now, and their inner being is changed. This is incredible news, and a truth we should embrace strongly. The idea that we're just forgiven, and that's all, is far from what God says. We are so much more than just forgiven; we are brand new creatures in Christ with a new nature and heart.

The Good News Entails Receiving a New Nature

Believers are also given a new nature. Yes, they still

retain their sinful nature, but they now have a brand-new nature as well that is much more powerful than their old sinful nature. In fact, the saved are blessed with all spiritual blessings in heavenly places:

Ephesians 1:3–4: *Blessed be the God and Father of our Lord Jesus Christ, who has **blessed us with every spiritual blessing in the heavenly places in Christ**, 4 just as He chose us in Him before the foundation of the world, that we would be holy and blameless before Him.*

Romans 6:4: *We were buried therefore with him by baptism into death, in order that, just as Christ was raised from the dead by the glory of the Father, we too might walk in **newness of life**.*

The Good News Entails Receiving a New Heart

Besides being born again, being a new creation in Christ, and possessing a new nature, a saved person is also given a new heart by God:

Ezekiel 36:26: *And I will give you a **new heart**, and a **new spirit** I will put within you. And I will **remove the heart of stone** from your flesh and give you a **heart of flesh**.*

The Good News Entails Being More Than Conquerors Over Sin

Romans 6:7–11: *For one who has died has been **set free from sin**. 8 Now if we have died with Christ, we believe that we will also live with him. 9 We know that Christ, being* *raised from the dead, will never die again; death no longer has dominion over him. 10 For the death he died he died to sin, once for all, but the life he lives he lives to God. 11 So you also must consider yourselves* **dead to sin and alive to God** *in Christ Jesus.*

Romans 8:36-37: *Who shall separate us from the love of Christ? Shall tribulation, or distress, or persecution, or famine, or nakedness, or danger, or sword? 36 As it is written, "For your sake we are being killed all the day long; we are regarded as sheep to be slaughtered." 37 No, in all these things we are* **more than conquerors** *through him who loved us.*

Now while the saved person still has the old sinful nature, they are no longer a slave to it. It no longer has power over them. They are more than conquerors over their sin through Christ. Christ now indwells the believer and has given them all they need to overcome and be victorious over sin. This is certainly good news to us, and those with whom we share the gospel.

The Good News Entails Healing from Past Sins

The wages of sin is death! Sin destroys, kills, ruins, and stains everyone who has walked in its path. When we are born again, we start a new life, and God helps us rebuild all that which sin has destroyed in our lives. Things like broken relationships, destructive habits, wrong ways of thinking, and wrong behavior can all change.

God can restore our life little by little to the way He intended it to be in the first place:

Joel 2:25-27: *So I will **restore to you the years that the swarming locust has eaten**, the crawling locust, the consuming locust, and the chewing locust, my great army which I sent among you. 26 You shall eat in plenty and be satisfied, and praise the name of the Lord your God, who has dealt wondrously with you; and My people shall never be put to shame. 27 Then you shall know that I am in the midst of Israel: I am the Lord your God and there is no other. My people shall never be put to shame.*

The good news brings hope for a better life and healing from sin's destruction. It's a life that is now pleasing and brings satisfaction to God, others, and even ourselves. It brings peace and goodness to our lives, and the years that sin destroyed, God can restore and rebuild for us.

The Good News Entails Purpose, Meaning, Love, Hope, and Joy

Our greatest needs, such as forgiveness, purpose in life, meaning, love, hope, joy, spiritual healing, having healthy relationships with others, and being right with our Creator and in fellowship with Him, is now possible.

The good news is beyond belief and truly the greatest news that has ever been given!

Chapter 5: What Is the Gospel: The Good News

Conclusion

The good news shines bright as a result of accurately sharing the bad news. If we fail to share the bad news, then the good news is diminished and devalued.

Christ has paid the price for our sins, and we can stand right before Him with all confidence, not because of anything we have done, but because of what He did for us on the Cross.

The gift of salvation not only includes eternal life with God in heaven, but life in the here and now. When we are born again, we become new creatures in Christ, are given a new nature, a new heart, a new spirit, and are more than conquerors in Christ.

Christ said He came to give us life and life in abundance: *"The thief comes only to steal and kill and destroy; I came that they **may have life, and have it abundantly**"* (John 10:10).

This doesn't mean we won't have difficulties, pain, suffering, persecution, trials, and so forth. But in it all, we have purpose, meaning, forgiveness, healing, restoration, joy, hope, love, and peace with God.

The gospel contains such great news that it's really beyond full comprehension. It's what every person should long for and desire. And it's such good news that we should shout it out to the world!

Chapter 6

What Must We Believe to Be Saved?

Chapter 6: What Must We Believe to Be Saved?

Terminology God Uses in Salvation

God uses several phrases to describe what we must understand and believe to be saved. Phrases such as *believe in Christ, follow Me, repent,* and *receive Christ* are all used interchangeably.

I don't think it's necessary to get hung up on what words or phrases we use. The above terms are all biblical and can be used as you see fit. Saying the right word or phrase is not what saves us. As long as we have a biblical understanding of salvation, it's the sincerity of our hearts that matter most.

In this chapter, we'll look at the key verses we must understand and believe to be saved.

We Must Believe Salvation Is a Free Gift

There is nothing we can do to earn salvation. It's absolutely free, and not through human effort in any way. We cannot do enough good deeds or anything else to earn it. It's by grace through faith and not by works:

Ephesians 2:8-9: *For by **grace** you have been saved through faith. And this is **not your own doing**; it is the **gift of God**, 9 **not a result of works**, so that no one may boast.*

Notice some keywords in this verse: ***grace, faith, gift of God,*** and ***works.***

What Is the Gospel and How to Share It

Grace is God's goodness and blessing that is based solely in His nature and not upon who we are or what we do or have done.

Faith is what we as humans exercise in salvation. It's our response to God's grace. Faith is not a work that earns salvation; it's just the means by which we believe and receive it.

A gift is something freely given and not earned. If salvation is earned, it ceases to be a gift and becomes something owed or a reward. Salvation is a gift freely given by God, and we must believe this in order to be saved:

Romans 6:23: *For the wages of sin is death, but the free gift of God is eternal life in Christ Jesus our Lord.*

Works are what some believe earn salvation. They believe if we follow certain rules, obey what our religion says, do enough good deeds, and so forth, then we are saved. God says there is nothing we can do to earn salvation, and we must believe this truth.

We stand right before God based solely upon what Christ did for us on the Cross, not what we do. Therefore, works done to earn salvation is what Scripture calls a "false gospel." However, works done as the result of salvation is what Scripture calls "fruit or works." Works, therefore, are the result of our salvation, not what earns it.

Chapter 6: What Must We Believe to Be Saved?

Salvation is a gift, but if not received through faith, then it has no value and is not applied to us. Therefore, there's just one simple response on our part in salvation; we must exercise faith to receive Christ's gift.

Because faith plays such a large role in salvation, we will be discussing in detail its characteristics in the following chapter.

We Must Believe Jesus Is Lord

Salvation must include a basic understanding of Jesus, and who He is, in order to believe in Him and receive salvation:

John 8:24: *Therefore, I said to you that you will die in your sins; for **unless you believe that I am He**, you will die in your sins.*

The phrase, *"Unless you believe I am He,"* means that we must believe that Jesus is Lord and the Messiah who came to earth to be the sacrifice for our sins. We also must believe that Jesus was God in the flesh and, therefore, has the authority to forgive our sins:

John 1:12–13: *But as many as received Him, to them He gave the right to become children of God, even to those who **believe in His name**, 13 who were born, not of blood nor of the will of the flesh nor of the will of man, but of God.*

John 3:36: *He who **believes in the Son** has eternal life; but he who does not obey the Son will not see life, but the wrath of God abides on him.*

1 Corinthians 15:1–5: *Now I make known to you, brethren, the* **gospel which I preached to you,** *which also you received, in which also you stand, 2* **by which also you are saved,** *if you hold fast the word which I preached to you, unless you believed in vain. 3 For I delivered to you as of first importance what I also received, that* **Christ died for our sins** *according to the Scriptures, 4 and that* **He was buried,** *and that* **He was raised** *on the third day according to the Scriptures, 5 and that He appeared to Cephas [Peter], then to the twelve.*

In this passage, we see two truths we must believe to be saved: (1) we must believe Christ died for our sins, and (2) Christ was buried and rose from the dead. Rising from the dead affirms that Jesus was who He claimed to be (God in the flesh) and was victorious over sin and death.

We Must Confess Christ as Lord and Believe God Raised Him from the Dead

Romans 10:8–11: *But what does it say? "The word is near you, in your mouth and in your heart" – that is, the word of faith which we are preaching, 9 that if you* **confess with your mouth Jesus as Lord,** *and* **believe in your heart that God raised Him from the dead, you will be saved;** *10 for with the heart a person believes, resulting in righteousness, and with the mouth he confesses, resulting in salvation. 11 For the Scripture says, "Whoever believes in Him will not be disappointed."*

Chapter 6: What Must We Believe to Be Saved?

In this passage, we see two truths we must believe and express in salvation: (1) We must believe and confess that Jesus is Lord. This also means we are acknowledging Him as the Lord of our lives and are willing to submit to His lordship. (2) We must believe that God raised Jesus from the dead. Again, rising from the dead means that Jesus was who He claimed to be and has the authority to be our sacrificial Lamb who died in our place to take away our sins and give us eternal life.

The Meaning of Believe

In the Hebrew culture of the Bible, the word *believe* had a different meaning than what we understand today. Let's look at the role of rabbis and their disciples during the time of Christ to glean understanding in this area.

As a disciple learned from their rabbi, they were placing their entire trust and belief in him. This process was called *believing*. Unlike today, the term *believe* had a very different meaning in the Hebrew culture. The Semitic understanding of *believe* was not based on an intellectual assent to a creed, doctrinal statement, or series of faith propositions. Rather, to a first-century disciple, *believe* is a verb in which you willingly submitted to your rabbi's interpretive authority regarding God's word in every area of your life. Thus, to say you were a disciple in the name of Gamaliel, meant that you totally surrendered your life to Gamaliel's way of interpreting Scripture. As a result, you conformed all of your life's behavior to his interpretations.[2]

The word *believe* in the Hebrew culture meant taking some action, applying knowledge to daily life, and changing some attitude or perspective, not just mentally knowing something and remaining unchanged.

Today, the word *believe* is used more as a noun and slants toward mere intellectual agreement or mental assent. This is a very different meaning than the usage in Christ's day. The fact that *believe* was understood as not only knowing something, but also as action and obedience is seen in how Jesus used the words interchangeably:

*He who **believes in the Son** has eternal life; but he who does **not obey the Son** will not see life, but the wrath of God abides on him* (John 3:36).

Notice what Jesus did not say in this verse, He didn't say: "*He who believes in the Son has eternal life; but he who does not [**Christ didn't use believe, but instead, obey**] in the Son will not see life, but the wrath of God*

---

[2] Doug Greenwold, *Being a First-Century Disciple*, 2007, Bible.org. https://bible.org/article/being-first-century-disciple. Accessed 08/14/2015.

abides on him."

If believe meant simply knowing something, Christ would have used believe both times in the verse, but He didn't. He used the word *obey* in place of *believe* in the second part of the verse. Therefore, according to Christ, believing also includes obedience, not just knowledge.

We Must Repent of Our Sins

What does repent mean? It means we change directions. It's going in a certain direction and then turning around and going in the opposite direction. Before salvation, the direction we are going is according to our own will, plans, purposes, dreams, and so forth. It means we are the lord of our lives and in control of the direction we want in life.

After salvation, the direction of our life changes 180 degrees and is based on Christ being our Lord. As a result, we now let Him be in control and choose the direction and plans He has for us.

Changing direction also includes sorrow for our sin and the selfish direction in which we were going.

Interestingly, in the preaching of John the Baptist and Jesus, repentance was their main theme:

Matthew 3:1-2: *Now in those days John the Baptist came, preaching in the wilderness of Judea, saying, 2* ***"Repent****, for the kingdom of heaven is at hand."*

Matthew 4:17: *From that time Jesus began to preach and say, "**Repent**, for the kingdom of heaven is at hand."*

Mark 1:14–15: *Now after John had been taken into custody, Jesus came into Galilee, preaching the gospel of God, 15 and saying, "The time is fulfilled, and the kingdom of God is at hand; **repent** and **believe in the gospel**."*

Because repentance plays such a critical role in salvation, let's look at some biblical characteristics of genuine repentance.

1. Biblical Repentance Acknowledges and Confesses Sin

Psalm 32:4–5: *For day and night Your hand was heavy upon me; my vitality was drained away as with the fever heat of summer.* **I acknowledged my sin to You, and my iniquity I did not hide**; *I said,* **"I will confess my transgressions to the Lord"**; *and You forgave the guilt of my sin.*

Those demonstrating biblical repentance will acknowledge and confess their sins to the Lord. If this is not done sincerely, then genuine repentance likely has not occurred.

2. Biblical Repentance Entails Godly Sorrow

2 Corinthians 7:8–11: *For though* **I caused you sorrow** *by my letter, I do not regret it; though I did regret it — for I see that that letter caused you* **sorrow**, *though only for a while 9 I now rejoice, not that you were made* **sorrowful**,

Chapter 6: What Must We Believe to Be Saved?

*but that you were made **sorrowful to the point of repentance**; for you were made **sorrowful according to the will of God**, so that you might not suffer loss in anything through us. 10 **For the sorrow that is according to the will of God produces a repentance without regret**, leading to salvation, but the sorrow of the world produces death. 11 For behold what earnestness this very thing, this **godly sorrow**, has produced in you: what **vindication** of yourselves, what **indignation**, what **fear**, what **longing**, what **zeal**, what **avenging of wrong**!*

Notice in verse 10 that there are two kinds of sorrow: (1) godly sorrow that produces repentance, and (2) worldly sorrow that produces death. Godly sorrow is sincere, humble, genuine, and willing to turn from sin to God and change behavior. Worldly sorrow just regrets the consequences, pain, and suffering sin causes but has no willingness to repent and turn to God.

We also see that biblical, godly sorrow will have vindication (being cleared of wrong), indignation (repudiation of sin), fear (fear of the Lord and what He thinks), longing (desiring that which is good), zeal (passion to serve and obey God), and avenging of wrong (restitution and restoration of wrongs committed). Biblical repentance is sorrow bathed in action and change, not just feeling bad.

3. Biblical Repentance Is Humble, Submissive, and Mournful

James 4:6–10: *Therefore, it says, "**God is opposed to the proud, but gives grace to the humble.**" **Submit, therefore to God.** Resist the devil and he will flee from you. **Draw near to God** and He will draw near to you. **Cleanse your hands**, you sinners; and **purify your hearts**, you double-minded. Be **miserable and mourn and weep; let your laughter be turned into mourning and your joy to gloom**. Humble yourselves in the presence of the Lord, and He will exalt you.*

Biblical repentance includes humility, submission to God, drawing near to God, cleansing, forsaking sin, purity of heart, mourning and sorrow, and weeping and gloom over sins committed. Repentance that does not genuinely include these attitudes is not biblical.

4. Biblical Repentance Bears Fruit

Matthew 3:7–8: *But when he [John the Baptist] saw many of the Pharisees and Sadducees coming for baptism, he said to them, "You brood of vipers, who warned you to flee from the wrath to come? 8 Therefore **bear fruit in keeping with repentance**."*

Biblical repentance should manifest itself with fruit. If there is no change of heart, change of will, change of direction in life, and no willingness to make Christ Lord, then sincere repentance has not occurred.

Chapter 6: What Must We Believe to Be Saved?

We Must Choose to Follow Christ

One of Christ's most used phrases in the call of salvation was, "*Follow Me.*" This phrase encompasses and summarizes what it means to believe, receive, repent, and make Christ Lord of our lives. It infers submission, obedience, lordship, and service to Christ.

Mark 8:34-35: *And He summoned the crowd with His disciples, and said to them, "If anyone wishes to **come after Me**, he must deny himself, and take up his cross and **follow Me**. 35 For whoever wishes to save his life will lose it, but whoever loses his life for My sake and the gospel's will save it."*

Matthew 19:21: *Jesus said to him, "If you wish to be complete, go and sell your possessions and give to the poor, and you will have treasure in heaven; and come, **follow Me**."*

John 12:26: *If anyone serves Me, he must **follow Me**; and where I am, there My servant will be also; if anyone serves Me, the Father will honor him.*

Matthew 4:18-20: *Now as Jesus was walking by the Sea of Galilee, He saw two brothers, Simon who was called Peter, and Andrew his brother, casting a net into the sea; for they were fishermen. 19 And He said to them, "**Follow Me**, and I will make you fishers of men." 20 Immediately they left their nets and **followed Him**.*

Following Christ means we no longer follow our own will, but Christ's will for us. It entails making

Christ the Lord of our lives and doing what He says, not what we want. It's surrender, yielding, obeying, and serving.

It was Christ's most used phrase because it encompasses and summarizes what it means to believe in Christ, receive Christ, repent of our sins, and make Christ Lord of our lives. It's the gospel message in a nutshell.

We Must Receive Christ As Savior

John 1:12–13: *But as many as **received Him**, to them He gave the right to become children of God, even to those who believe in His name, 13 who were born, not of blood nor of the will of the flesh nor of the will of man, but of God.*

Salvation is worthless unless received. We must not only believe certain truths about Christ and salvation, but we must receive Christ to be saved. Therefore, the term, ***receive Christ as Savior and Lord,*** is probably the most used phrase in the call of salvation today.

Conclusion

Salvation is absolutely free and cannot be earned. Faith is the vehicle through which we receive God's free gift of salvation. Our faith is based upon understanding and believing certain truths, and we cannot have biblical faith without knowing them. Therefore, biblical faith is built upon the truth of God's word and what He says about salvation.

Chapter 6: What Must We Believe to Be Saved?

When we come to understand the basic truths about salvation, we are then in a position to act upon this knowledge. Acting upon this knowledge is what the Bible calls faith or believing.

Biblical faith and believing, according to the verses we've looked at in this chapter, should include the following understandings, beliefs, and expressions:

- We must understand and believe salvation is a free gift and cannot be earned (Eph. 2:8-9; Rom. 6:23).
- We must understand and believe Jesus is Lord and Messiah (John 1:12-13; John 3:36; 1 Cor. 15:1-5).
- We must understand and confess Christ as Lord, and believe He died on the Cross, was buried, and rose from the dead to pay for our sins and give us eternal life (Rom. 10:8-11; 1 Cor. 15:1-5).
- We must understand and genuinely repent of our sins and turn to Christ (Matt. 3:7-8; James 4:6-10).
- We must understand and choose to follow Christ as the Lord of our lives (Mark 8:34-35; Matt. 19:21; John 12:26; Matt. 4:18-19).
- We must understand, believe, and receive Christ as our personal Lord and Savior (John 1:12-13).

What we do in believing and expressing our faith in salvation should not be confused as works that earn salvation. It's just what we do in receiving salvation. Salvation is a gift, but unless received through faith and believing, it has no value, and is not applied to us.

Chapter 7

What Is Saving Faith?

Chapter 7: What Is Saving Faith?

Is it possible to be saved, yet have no works or expression of faith in our lives? Is belief in God enough to save us, or must some measure of fruit accompany our faith to be genuine, saving faith? Is salvation without any expression or evidence biblical?

Because we are saved by grace through faith (Eph. 2:8-9), it's vital we understand what saving faith is.

We Are Saved by Grace Through Faith

Faith is the vehicle through which we believe and receive salvation: *"For by grace you have been **saved through faith**. And this is not your own doing; it is the gift of God, 9 not a result of works, so that no one may boast"* (Eph. 2:8-9).

God makes it clear that salvation is a gift received through faith. Our faith is what we exercise in the salvation process. What we do in expressing our faith should not be confused as works that earn salvation. It's just what we do in receiving salvation. Salvation is a free gift, but unless received through faith, it has no value and is not applied to us.

It's helpful to separate what God does in salvation from what the human agent's response is to that salvation. God provides salvation as a free gift based solely on what Christ did on the Cross for us. His death, burial, and resurrection are the payment for our sins. We can add nothing to it, and salvation is totally free through Jesus Christ.

However, in order to receive this free gift, the human agent must receive it through faith. For this reason, in this chapter we'll focus on what biblical, saving faith is, and the Scriptural ways it's expressed or evidenced.

Saving Faith Is an Obedient Faith

Is salvation without any obedience, saving faith and biblical?

Dallas Willard quotes a statement by A. W. Tozer concerning the belief in salvation without obedience: "A notable heresy has come into being throughout Evangelical Christian circles—the widely accepted concept that we humans can choose to accept Christ only because we need him as Savior and that we have the right to postpone our obedience to Him as Lord as long as we want to!"[3] Willard then goes on to state that "Salvation apart from obedience is unknown in the sacred scriptures. This 'heresy' has created the impression that it is quite reasonable to be a 'Vampire Christian.' One in effect says to Jesus, 'I'd like a little of your blood, please, but I don't care to be your student or have your character. In fact, won't you just excuse

---

[3] A. W. Tozer, *I Call It Heresy*, Harrisburg, Penn, Christian Publications, 1974, p. 5, quoted by Dallas Willard, 2009-10-13, *The Great Omission*, HarperCollins. Kindle Edition, p. 229.

Chapter 7: What Is Saving Faith?

me while I get on with my life and I'll see you in heaven?'" [4]

John MacArthur has also spoken out about what he believes is a misunderstanding regarding the relationship between salvation and obedience. He claims that some theologians have proposed a gospel wherein one can receive eternal life yet continue to live in rebellion against God.[5] He notes, "They've been told that the only criterion for salvation is knowing and believing some basic facts about Christ. They hear from the beginning that obedience is optional."[6] MacArthur refutes this belief by asserting, "The gospel Jesus proclaimed was a call to discipleship, a call to follow Him in submissive obedience, not just a plea to make a decision or pray a prayer."[7]

For those who think we can be saved, and then live as we please, Christ has a sobering warning: *"Not everyone who says to me,* **'Lord, Lord,'** *will enter the kingdom of heaven, but the one who* **does the will of my Father** *who is in heaven"* (Matt. 7:21).

Christ warns that it's not those who call Him "Lord" who will be saved, but those who do the will of His

---

[4] Dallas Willard, *The Great Omission* (HarperCollins. Kindle Edition, 2009-10-13), pp. 13-14.
[5] John MacArthur, *The Gospel According to Jesus* ((Grand Rapids, Michigan, Zondervan Publishing House, 1988), p. 15.
[6] Ibid., p. 17.
[7] Ibid., p. 21.

Father. He asserts that it's not what a person says, but what they do that matters, and that it's possible to acknowledge Him as Lord, but not be genuinely saved. This verse counters the argument of some who believe we can be saved, yet not obey. Christ stresses that true faith is active and should include obedience to be saving faith. He claims that mere mental assent does not save, but that saving faith must be expressed by obedience to be genuine.

Notice also that Christ says, *"On that day many will say to me, 'Lord, Lord, did we not prophesy in your name, and cast out demons in your name, and **do many mighty works in your name?**' And then will I declare to them, 'I never knew you; depart from me, you workers of lawlessness'"* (Matt. 7:22-23).

Christ states that many will not enter the Kingdom of Heaven because they are basing their salvation on works, not faith. They believe their "mighty works" will save them, not their faith in Christ alone and a relationship with Him. Christ warns us that salvation is not by works but by grace.

We find, then, two factors that can result in false salvation: (1) Belief in God without obedience, and (2) basing our salvation on works and not grace. Christ warns of both dangers in Matthew 7:21-23.

Now while genuine saving faith should be accompanied by works of some sort, we should clarify

Chapter 7: What Is Saving Faith?

that this doesn't imply perfection. It can be hard sometimes to determine what level of expression our faith should have, but according to Christ, saving faith should have some element of obedience to be sincere. For the person who claims to be saved, yet lives in stark disobedience to God, then it would be safe to say that they did not have genuine saving faith, and as a result, their salvation is in question.

Saving Faith and the Role of Obedience

Christ taught that genuine salvation should result in obedience:

John 3:36: *Whoever **believes** in the Son has eternal life; whoever **does not obey** the Son shall not see life, but the wrath of God remains on him.*

Interestingly, Christ uses the word ***believe*** as synonymous with ***obey***. According to Christ, believing is obeying, and obeying is believing. They are one and the same.

In this text, it's safe to say that some level of obedience to the Son is necessary for receiving eternal life, and without it, we are not genuinely saved. Salvation is a free gift given by grace through faith in Christ, but the fruit, or evidence of salvation according to Christ, is obedience.

What Is the Gospel and How to Share It

Saving Faith and the Sermon on the Mount

Another powerful example regarding the importance of obedience in relation to salvation is found at the end of the Sermon on the Mount:

Matthew 7:24–27: *Everyone then who hears these words of mine and **does them** will be like a wise man who built his house on the rock. And the rain fell, and the floods came, and the winds blew and beat on that house, but it did not fall, because it had been founded on the rock. And everyone who hears these words of mine and **does not do them** will be like a foolish man who built his house on the sand. And the rain fell, and the floods came, and the winds blew and beat against that house, and it fell, and great was the fall of it.*

The difference between the salvation or destruction of each house (people's lives) in the parable rested upon whether or not they obeyed Christ's words or just heard them.

Now the significance of this passage is weighty. The Sermon on the Mount is the longest sermon recorded in the Gospels that Christ preached. Some theologians have equated the Mount of Beatitudes (the location where Christ preached the Sermon on the Mount) with the Old Covenant given on Mt. Sinai. Some scholars believe that in the same way God gave the summation of the Old Covenant on Mt. Sinai, Christ gave the summation of the New Covenant on the Mount of Beatitudes.

Chapter 7: What Is Saving Faith?

If the summation of the New Covenant entails the importance of doing and obeying what Christ taught, then it would seem logical that the gospel message of salvation would include the same. Therefore, a gospel message that permits mental belief only in God, and excludes the need for some level of obedience, would fall far short of what Christ proclaimed.

Saving Faith and the Parable of the Sower

Christ also spoke about the marks of a genuine believer in the Parable of the Sower (Matt. 13:1-23). A sower sowed seed (God's word) upon four different kinds of soils (people's hearts). The first soil rejected the seed, and the next two soils showed life for a bit, but then died and didn't produce fruit. It was only the soil that produced fruit that was truly saved. According to Christ, the mark of a genuine believer is fruit, not just belief in God.

Saving Faith and a Rich Young Man

Christ engaged a rich young man who knew much of the Bible, believed in God, had much of Scripture memorized, and even kept many of the Ten Commandments, yet wasn't saved. Jesus used this encounter to teach that salvation without making Christ Lord of our lives and following Him, is not saving faith. Matthew 19 recounts the meeting:

What Is the Gospel and How to Share It

Matthew 19:16–22: *And behold, a man came up to him, saying, "Teacher, what good deed **must I do to have eternal life**?" And he said to him, "Why do you ask me about what is good? There is only one who is good. If you would enter life, keep the commandments." He said to him, "Which ones?" And Jesus said, "you shall not murder, you shall not commit adultery, you shall not steal, you shall not bear false witness, honor your father and mother, and, you shall love your neighbor as yourself." The young man said to him, "All these I have kept. What do I still lack?" Jesus said to him, "If you would be perfect, go, sell what you possess and give to the poor, and you will have treasure in heaven; **and come, follow me**." When the young man heard this, he went away sorrowful, for he had great possessions.*

Interestingly, the rich young man knew he wasn't saved, and Jesus knew it as well. There was no debate about that. However, despite the rich young man's knowledge of God, belief in Him, and obedience to some of the Ten Commandments, he wasn't saved. He lacked one thing: he was unwilling to submit to Christ's lordship and follow Him. He rejected Christ and chose to remain the lord of his own life.

This passage indicates that belief in God, and even some Christian activity, isn't enough to save us. Faith must be accompanied by acknowledging the lordship of Christ to be genuine, saving faith. If we refuse to recognize Christ as our Lord, and instead, remain the

Chapter 7: What Is Saving Faith?

lords of our own lives, this reveals that repentance and genuine salvation are in question.

Saving Faith and the Family of God

After a long session of teaching about the Parables of the Kingdom, in which Christ had emphasized the importance of putting His words into practice instead of just hearing them, Christ was told that His mother and brothers were seeking Him. His response to them was quite fascinating:

Luke 8:21: *But he answered them, "My mother and my brothers are those who **hear the word of God and do it.**"*

Christ states that it's those who do His words that are part of His family, not those who merely hear His words without doing them. He stresses that saving faith should be accompanied by obedience to be sincere and biblical.

Saving Faith and Mere Knowledge

Christ continually warned that hearing without obeying brings greater condemnation because we know what to do but refuse to do it. The following passage speaks of those who heard Christ's words but chose not to repent and obey them:

Matthew 11:20–24: *Then He began to denounce the cities in which most of His miracles were done, because they **did not repent**. "Woe to you, Chorazin! Woe to you, Bethsaida! For if the mighty works done in you had been* *done in Tyre and Sidon, they would have repented long ago in sackcloth and ashes. But I tell you, it will be more bearable on the day of judgment for Tyre and Sidon than for you. And you, Capernaum, will you be exalted to heaven? You will be brought down to Hades. For if the mighty works done in you had been done in Sodom, it would have remained until this day. But I tell you that it will be more tolerable on the day of judgment for the land of Sodom than for you."*

Throughout the whole of Scripture, we see biblical faith that is obedient always brings blessings from God, but mere mental assent without obedience always brings His judgment.

For example, the reason the nation of Israel was deported to Assyria and Babylon was because of their lack of obedience. Most Israelites believed in God; they just didn't obey Him. Their mere belief in Him did not save them from being deported and escaping judgment.

Saving Faith and the Book of James

The main theme of the Book of James strives to define faith and works, otherwise known as belief and fruit. It clarifies what genuine faith is and how it's expressed. It's not teaching that works save us, but that true faith should include fruit that provides evidence of salvation.

James 2:14-26 is devoted to answering the question about the relationship between faith and works. It

Chapter 7: What Is Saving Faith?

begins with the question about what kind of faith is saving faith:

James 2:14: *What use is it, my brethren, if someone says he has faith, but he has no works?* ***Can that faith save him?***

This verse squarely centers on answering what kind of faith is genuine, saving faith.

Because this truth is so important, God provides five examples to show us what saving faith embodies. As already noted, when God repeatedly says something, it means He wants to embed that truth deep into our hearts.

Example 1: *If a brother or sister is without clothing and in need of daily food, 16 and one of you says to them, Go in peace, be warmed and be filled, and yet you do not give them what is necessary for their body, what use is that? 17* ***Even so, faith, if it has no works, is dead, being by itself*** (Jam. 2:15-17).

According to God, faith that is not expressed by action is dead and is not saving faith.

Example 2: *But someone may well say, "You have faith, and I have works; show me your faith without the works, and* ***I will show you my faith by my works****"* (Jam. 2:18).

Again, God clarifies that faith without any expression of action is not saving faith. There must be some evidence, or it's not genuine.

Example 3: *You believe that God is one. You do well; the demons also believe, and shudder. 20 But are you willing to recognize, you foolish fellow, that **faith without works is useless**?* (Jam. 2:19-20).

Notice that despite believing in God and shuddering, the demons are not saved. This proves that mere belief in God does not save us, and that faith must have some expression of obedience to be genuine, saving faith. If our belief has no works, it's just mere knowledge and is useless.

Example 4: *Was not Abraham our father justified by works when he offered up Isaac his son on the altar? 22 You see that **faith was working with his works**, and as a **result of the works, faith was perfected**; 23 and the Scripture was fulfilled which says, "And Abraham believed God, and it was reckoned to him as righteousness," and he was called the friend of God. 24 You see that a man is **justified by works and not by faith alone*** (Jam. 2:21-24).

These verses might seem contrary to Ephesians 2:8-9, that says we are saved by grace and not works, but they're not. God is stressing that faith must be expressed by fruit to be genuine, saving faith. Note how it says, *"Abraham **believed** God, and it was **reckoned to him as righteousness**."* Abraham's belief was expressed in action; he not only knew what to do, but he did it.

Chapter 7: What Is Saving Faith?

Example 5: *In the same way, was not Rahab the harlot also justified by works when she received the messengers and sent them out by another way? 26* **For just as the body without the spirit is dead, so also faith without works is dead** (Jam. 2:25-26).

Again, God is stressing that our works provide evidence of faith. If we have no works, then our faith is dead and useless, and is not biblical.

In these five examples of faith, God clearly defines that genuine, saving faith must be accompanied by some level of works (fruit) to be true faith, and if not, it's dead and cannot save us.

For those who claim that belief is enough for salvation, John MacArthur boldly responds: "The faith they are relying on is only intellectual acquiescence to a set of facts. It will not save."[8]

I think it's worth noting that in Christianity, we have done a good job defining that salvation is by grace through faith and not of works. However, I would suggest that we haven't done a very good job of clarifying what genuine, saving faith entails.

---

[8] John MacArthur, *The Gospel According to Jesus* (Grand Rapids, Michigan, Zondervan Publishing House, 1988), p. 170.

Saving Faith and Examples from Scripture

What is true faith according to Scripture? Is it only mental belief about certain facts, or does it entail more?

In Hebrews 11, we find the longest and fullest treatise on the definition and example of biblical faith. Note how each expression of faith possesses a verb of action:

- By faith, Noah **built** an ark.
- By faith, Abraham **obeyed** and left his country to follow God to the Promised Land.
- By faith, Sarah **received** power to conceive.
- By faith, Abraham, when he was tested, **offered up** Isaac.
- By faith, Isaac **invoked** future blessings on Jacob and Esau.
- By faith, Jacob, when dying, **blessed** each of the sons of Joseph.
- By faith, Joseph, at the end of his life, **made mention** of the exodus of the Israelites and **gave directions** concerning his bones.
- By faith, Moses, when he was born, **was hidden** for three months by his parents.
- By faith, Moses, when he was grown up, **refused** to be called the son of Pharaoh's daughter, **choosing** rather to be mistreated with the people of God than to enjoy the fleeting pleasures of sin.

Chapter 7: What Is Saving Faith?

- By faith, Moses **kept** the Passover and sprinkled the blood so that the Destroyer of the firstborn might not touch them.
- By faith, the people **crossed** the Red Sea as on dry land.
- By faith, the walls of Jericho **fell** after the Israelites had **encircled** them for seven days.
- By faith, Rahab the prostitute did not perish with those who were disobedient because she had **given** a friendly welcome to the spies.
- By faith, Gideon, Barak, Samson, Jephthah, David, Samuel, and the prophets **conquered** kingdoms, **enforced** justice, **obtained** promises, **stopped** the mouths of lions, **quenched** the power of fire, **escaped** the edge of the sword, were **made** strong out of weakness, became **mighty** in war, and put foreign armies to **flight**.
- By faith, women **received** back their dead by resurrection; some were tortured, **refusing** to accept release so that they might rise again to a better life.
- By faith, others **suffered** mocking and flogging, and even chains and imprisonment, they were stoned, they were sawn in two, they were killed with the sword, they **went about** in skins of sheep and goats, destitute, afflicted, and mistreated.

The fascinating truth about all these examples of

faith is that they are characterized by action. Their faith was followed by doing something, not mere static belief. Each example is followed by a verb, a verb of action, a verb of obedience. Each person displayed works that bore witness to their faith.

Now once again, it's critical we clarify the difference between works done to earn salvation and works done as the result of salvation. Works done to earn salvation is what Scripture calls a "false gospel." Works done as the result of salvation is what Scripture calls "fruit or works." Works, therefore, are the result of our salvation, not what earns it. However, if our faith does not have works and fruit, it is dead and not saving faith.

Saving Faith and John the Baptist

John the Baptist strongly rebuked those in his day who thought they could just believe in God and not bear fruit:

Matthew 3:7–10: *But when he saw many of the Pharisees and Sadducees coming to his baptism, he said to them, "You brood of vipers! Who warned you to flee from the wrath to come?* **Bear fruit in keeping with repentance.** *And do not presume to say to yourselves, 'We have Abraham as our father,' for I tell you, God is able from these stones to raise up children for Abraham. Even now the axe is laid to the root of the trees. Every tree therefore that* **does not bear good fruit is cut down and thrown into the fire.**"

Chapter 7: What Is Saving Faith?

This passage clearly teaches that faith without fruit is not saving faith.

Saving Faith and Following Jesus

Christ's most used phrase in calling people to salvation was, "*Follow Me.*"

Mark 8:34: *And He summoned the crowd with His disciples, and said to them, "If anyone wishes to **come after Me**, he must deny himself, and take up his cross and **follow Me**.*

The term *follow Me* is a call to action. It's a verb and entails more than belief. In a practical sense, following Christ cannot be done without some kind of action on our part. We cannot follow Christ if we are unwilling to submit to His lordship and obey Him.

Saving Faith and Fruit

Christ spoke about true and false prophets, and how we'd know the difference between them:

Matthew 7:15–20: *Beware of false prophets, who come to you in sheep's clothing but inwardly are ravenous wolves. You will recognize them by their fruits. Are grapes gathered from thornbushes, or figs from thistles? So, every healthy tree bears good fruit, but the diseased tree bears bad fruit. A healthy tree cannot bear bad fruit, nor can a diseased tree bear good fruit. **Every tree that does not bear good fruit is cut down and thrown into the fire. Thus, you will recognize them by their fruits.***

Christ says the way we recognize genuine believers from false believers is by their fruits. He also said the false believers would be cut down and thrown into the fire. Therefore, those who don't produce fruit of genuine salvation are not true believers. According to Christ, it's the fruit of a person's life, not their mere belief in Him, that distinguishes a true believer from a false believer.

Saving Faith and Good Works

The most quoted verses on the foundational doctrine that salvation is by grace through faith in Christ and not by works is Ephesians 2:8-9:

For by grace you have been saved through faith. And this is not your own doing; it is the gift of God, 9 not a result of works, so that no one may boast.

However, many Christians disassociate Ephesians 2:8-9 from Ephesians 2:10. Ephesians 2:10 reveals what the result or outflow of Ephesians 2:8-9 should be:

*For we are his workmanship, created in Christ Jesus for **good works**, which God prepared beforehand, that we should walk in them.*

By seeing these verses together, we learn that salvation entails faith in God, and then results in an expression of works. Therefore, true faith should be evidenced by works in a believer's life if it is genuine, saving faith.

Chapter 7: What Is Saving Faith?

Saving Faith and the Fear of the Lord

The phrases *"fear the Lord"* and *"love the Lord"* go hand in hand. To love the Lord is to fear Him, and to fear the Lord is to love Him:

Psalm 103:11: *For as high as the heavens are above the earth, so great is his* ***steadfast love*** *toward those who* ***fear him***.

Psalm 103:17: *But the steadfast* ***love of the Lord*** *is from everlasting to everlasting on those who* ***fear him***, *and his righteousness to children's children.*

These verses show that the fear of the Lord and the love of the Lord are harmonious, not conflictive truths.

Christ defines, in large part, what it means to love God:

John 14:21: *Whoever has my commandments* ***and keeps them, he it is who loves me***. *And he who loves me will be loved by my Father, and I will love him and manifest myself to him.*

Keeping God's commandments is the mark of a person who truly loves and fears the Lord.

What is the fear of the Lord? It's a reverent awe of God's majesty and power that leads to a serious and sober desire to obey God in all matters. Therefore, a person who is genuinely saved will show their love and fear of the Lord through careful obedience. Their passion will be to seek the Lord's will for their life through God's word. They will be honest with the Scriptures and have no willingness to alter them to fit with their own desires or those of their culture.

Saving Faith and Discipleship

Despite the verses that teach salvation and obedience go hand in hand, some believe that obedience is optional, and that one can be saved without obeying and following Christ. I believe this misunderstanding is a significant factor leading to the neglect of discipleship today.

Many think that as long as they believe and have faith in God, they are saved. They cling to their belief as sufficient for salvation and believe bearing fruit and being a follower of Christ are optional. As a result, they usually have a low view of the importance of discipleship, and little or no growth happens in their lives.

Conclusion

I believe that according to Christ and the rest of Scripture, genuine salvation should result in fruit-bearing. We should desire to follow, be obedient, and submit to the lordship of our Master. True faith should produce fruit in our lives that bears witness to the fact that genuine salvation has occurred. The fruit produced doesn't save us but is a result of salvation.

Chapter 7: What Is Saving Faith?

The belief that we can be saved without bearing any fruit also negatively affects discipleship. If we believe we can be saved without being a disciple and bearing any fruit, then we run the risk of being false believers. We'll also neglect discipleship as our focus will not be on serving God, but on a false version of the gospel wherein we believe we can be saved but live as we wish with little or no accountability to God.

Genuine, saving faith should result in bearing fruit. It does not entail just mental assent and mere knowledge, but some action on our part that results in doing the will of God.

Saving faith doesn't mean we obey Christ perfectly and never sin, but that our faith is expressed and evidenced by some level of obedience.

Therefore, can a person be saved and not produce any fruit? I believe the answer is no. There should be some evidence of fruit. We're not talking about perfection, but some level of obedience. We must realize that genuine faith produces fruit, not the absence of it.

Chapter 8

How to Share the Gospel in Seven Clear Steps

Chapter 8: How to Share the Gospel in Seven Clear Steps

Having an evangelism guide that is clear, accurate, and articulates each aspect of the gospel can be an invaluable tool in sharing the gospel. That's the purpose of this chapter; to provide a seven-step evangelism guide that's easy to use.

If possible, it would be good to memorize these steps and a verse or two for each of the steps.

At the end of this chapter, a link is provided to our website where you can download and print free Bible tracts that follow the steps outlined in this chapter.

Step 1: God Loves Us

God is our Creator and longs to have a relationship with us because of His great love for us. He desires to save us from hell, give us life now, and that we would spend eternity in heaven with Him. He loves us with a jealous love and is deeply hurt when we reject Him, ignore Him, and live life without Him (Ex. 20:5).

We are His created children, and He yearns to be our Heavenly Father. He longs to care for us, provide for us, help us, protect us, bless us, direct our paths, and walk through life with us moment by moment:

Jeremiah 31:3: *The Lord appeared to him from afar, saying, "I have loved you with an everlasting love; therefore, I have **drawn you with lovingkindness**."*

John 3:16: *For God so **loved the world**, that he gave his only Son, that whoever believes in him should not perish but* *have eternal life.*

Ephesians 2:4-7: *But God, being rich in mercy, because of **His great love with which He loved us**, 5 even when we were dead in our transgressions, made us alive together with Christ (by grace you have been saved), 6 and raised us up with Him, and seated us with Him in the heavenly places in Christ Jesus, 7 so that in the ages to come He might show the **surpassing riches of His grace in kindness toward us in Christ Jesus**.*

Step 2: We Have Sinned and Are Separated from God

Our sin and rejection of God separate us from Him, the life He wants to give us now, and a future in heaven with Him. We have lost our relationship with God, our Creator, and as a result, have a sinful heart. We have transgressed God's laws of right and wrong and have followed our own sinful will instead. We do not desire to please God and have set ourselves up as the lord of our lives in place of God:

Genesis 2:15-17: *The Lord God took the man and put him in the Garden of Eden to work it and keep it. And the Lord God commanded the man, saying, "You may surely eat of every tree of the garden, but of the tree of the knowledge of good and evil you shall not eat, for in the day that you eat of it **you shall surely die**."*

The result of Adam and Eve's sin was a broken relationship with God:

Genesis 3:8: *They heard the sound of the Lord God*

walking in the garden in the cool of the day, and the man and his wife **hid themselves from the presence of the Lord God** among the trees of the garden.

Isaiah 59:2: *But your iniquities have made a* **separation between you and your God**, *and your sins have hidden his face from you so that he does not hear.*

Not only have we transgressed God's laws of right and wrong, but our greatest sin is being separated and not having a relationship with God our Creator. Because the greatest command is to love the Lord with all our heart, soul, mind, and strength, our greatest sin is not doing so. This is our primary sin.

As a result of the fall of Adam and Eve, sin has been passed on to everyone:

Romans 3:23: *For* **all have sinned** *and fall short of the glory of God.*

Step 3: The Consequences of Our Sin

The price for practicing sin and rejecting God is separation from Him for all eternity in hell:

Romans 6:23: *For the wages of sin is* **death**, *but the free gift of God is eternal life in Christ Jesus our Lord.*

Matthew 13:49–50: *So it will be at the end of the age. The angels will come out and separate the evil from the righteous and throw them into the* **fiery furnace**. *In that place there will be* **weeping and gnashing of teeth**.

Revelation 21:8: *But as for the cowardly, the faithless, the detestable, as for murderers, the sexually immoral, sorcerers, idolaters, and all liars, their portion will be in the **lake that burns with fire and sulfur**, which is the second death.*

Step 4: Christ Paid for Our Sins on the Cross

Christ's crucifixion on the Cross pays for our sins and removes them from us as far as the east is from the west. The penalty for sin, which is separation from God in hell for eternity, was paid for us by Christ. As a result, in Christ, our sins are forgiven, our shame removed, and we can now have a relationship with God and eternal life in heaven. Moreover, we can be healed from sin's consequences and experience abundant life in the present.

Isaiah 53:5: *But he was **pierced for our transgressions;** he was **crushed for our iniquities;** upon him was the chastisement that brought us peace, and with **his wounds we are healed.***

Psalm 103:12: *As far as the east is from the west, so far has **He removed our transgressions** from us.*

Romans 5:8: *But God shows his love for us in that while we were still sinners, **Christ died for us**.*

Romans 6:23: *For the wages of sin is death, but the **free gift of God is eternal life** in Christ Jesus our Lord.*

Ephesians 2:8–9: *For by grace **you have been saved**

Chapter 8: How to Share the Gospel in Seven Clear Steps

*through faith. And this is not your own doing; it is the **gift of God**, not a result of works, so that no one may boast.*

John 10:10: *The thief comes only to steal and kill and destroy; I came that they **may have life, and have it abundantly.***

Step 5: Response to the Gospel Message

After clearly sharing the gospel, it's appropriate to bring the person you're sharing with to the point of decision. A simple question like: "Would you like to receive Christ as your Savior and Lord and His gift of salvation? Depending on their response, here are some helpful verses to share with them:

John 1:12: *But to all who did **receive him, who believed in his name**, he gave the right to become children of God.*

John 3:36: *Whoever **believes in the Son** has eternal life; whoever does not obey the Son shall not see life, but the wrath of God remains on him.*

Acts 4:12: *And there is **salvation in no one else**, for there is no other name under heaven given among men by which we **must be saved**.*

Step 6: Receiving the Gift of Salvation

Following are the basic truths a person must understand and believe to be saved:

1. Believe salvation is free and cannot be earned.

2. Confess you are a sinner in need of Christ's offer of salvation through faith.
3. Believe that Jesus is Lord and died on the Cross to pay for your sins and rose from the dead to give you eternal life.
4. Repent and confess your sins to God, asking for His forgiveness and grace.
5. Give your heart and will to Christ, and choose to follow Him as the Lord of your life.

Helpful Prayer in Receiving Salvation

It's important to note that getting the words right in a prayer to be saved is not vital. God looks at the heart, and words are secondary. It's not a perfect prayer that saves us, but the sincerity of our heart that matters most.

Below is a suggested prayer you might use to help the person with whom you are sharing the gospel verbalize their prayer and heart to the Lord:

Thank you, Lord, for helping me understand my sinfulness and the reality of heaven and hell. I recognize that I am a sinner and deserve the punishment of eternity in hell as a result. I believe You died on the Cross and rose from the dead to pay the price for my sin and rebellion against You. I believe You are Lord and ask that You would forgive my sins against You. I repent of my sins and ask You to enter my heart and save me. Fill me with your Spirit and guide my life. I give you my heart and

Chapter 8: How to Share the Gospel in Seven Clear Steps

make you the Lord of my life. Grant me your grace to follow and obey You from now on. Thank you for hearing my prayer. Amen.

Step 7: What to Do Next

After the person you're sharing the gospel with has made their decision to believe in Christ and receive His gift of salvation, it would be wise to counsel them regarding some steps to take in beginning their new life in Christ and how to grow in Him.

1. Pray to God regularly and develop a relationship with Him.
2. Read or listen to the Bible daily.
3. Become part of a Bible-believing church that preaches God's word.
4. Get involved in a discipleship program.
5. Be baptized as soon as possible.
6. Be faithful to God and seek Him with all your heart.

Should You Tell a Person They Are Saved After Praying to Receive Christ?

My personal opinion is that I do not recommend telling people they are saved. As a pastor and missionary, I have seen countless people pray to receive Christ but not follow through with the Lord. In a short time, they aren't in church and are back to their regular lifestyle. I don't want to tell them they are saved and lead them to believe that just because they prayed a prayer, raised their hand, came to the front of the church, and so forth, that they are now saved. While I believe genuine salvation takes place in a moment of time, I also believe it takes time for saving faith to manifest itself.

As we saw in chapter 7, saving faith is expressed and evidenced by fruit. Therefore, it will take some time to see fruit. I don't want to assure a person who prays a prayer that they are saved when they might not be.

Only God knows if a person's prayer and heart are genuine or not in salvation. We simply can't see into the invisible realm and know what has happened in a person's heart. The only way we, as humans, can know this is by the fruit the person bears. Therefore, I don't believe it's wise to tell a person they are saved.

Additionally, I believe it's the Holy Spirit's job to confirm salvation in the heart of a person, not ours. Consider the following verses:

Romans 8:16: *The Spirit Himself testifies with our spirit that we are children of God.*

1 Corinthians 15:1–2: *Now I make known to you, brethren, the gospel which I preached to you, which also you received, in which also you stand, by which also you are saved, if you* **hold fast the word** *which I preached to you, unless you have believed in vain.*

Chapter 8: How to Share the Gospel in Seven Clear Steps

We also see in the Parable of the Sower that two soils (rocky and thorny) out of the four soils (responses to God's word) showed life for a bit but then fell away and died. The soils in this parable represent people's hearts and their responses to God's word. From the outside, it looked like these two soils were doing great and saved. However, after some time, they revealed through a lack of fruit and falling away that they indeed were not genuinely saved.

Therefore, for these reasons, I'm reluctant to assure people they are saved because it takes time to see if their response to the gospel is genuine or not.

Helpful Resources for Free Bible Tracts

If you would like access to free Bible tracts that follow the exact format as above, then we have these available on our GoMissionsToMexico.com website. These tracts can be downloaded and printed as you wish, and are generic tracts that can be used by anyone. If you want, you can stamp your name and contact info on the back, or the contact info of your church as well, or both if you'd like.

Just scroll down on the Trip Prep Section of the website to Box 9: "Training Resources ~ Get Ready for Cross-Cultural Ministry!" And at the bottom of the box, you will see two links to these free downloadable resources: www.gomissionstomexico.com/mission-trip-prep-section

Chapter 9

What to Do After Salvation?

Chapter 9: What to Do After Salvation?

After salvation, the next step in a believer's life is discipleship. Because this is so important, this chapter is devoted to understanding this vital truth.

What Is Discipleship?

Dallas Willard, in his book *The Great Omission*, makes an incredible observation regarding the importance of discipleship when stating that the word *disciple* occurs 269 times in the New Testament, but *Christian* is only found three times.[9] Willard defines discipleship as the foundational aspect of what it means to be saved and be a true follower of Christ.

Anthony Robinson, in his article "Follow Me," picks up on Willard's statement and believes that because the word *disciple* occurs 269 times in the New Testament, it defines the mark of a genuine believer.[10] Robinson also contends that the church today is focusing primarily on conversion and neglecting the way of life here and now, which is discipleship.[11]

Discipleship is the process of becoming like Christ in our nature, character, values, purposes, thoughts, knowledge, attitudes, and will. In other words, it's the

---

[9] Dallas Willard, *The Great Omission* (HarperCollins, Kindle Edition, 2009-10-13), p. 3.
[10] Anthony B. Robinson, *The Renewed Focus on Discipleship: 'Follow Me'* (Christian Century, 124 no 18 S 4 2007, pp. 23-25. Publication Type: Article. ATLA Religion Database with ATLASerials. Hunter Resource Library), p. 23, Accessed 12/10/2014.
[11] Ibid., p. 23.

process of becoming spiritually mature. It lasts a lifetime and isn't relegated to a temporary study or dedicated class taken for a time and ended. Bill Hull claims, "It's not a program or an event; it's a way of life. Discipleship is not for beginners alone; it's for all believers for every day of their lives."[12]

Discipleship Is the Only Way to Spiritual Maturity

Discipleship is the vehicle God uses to make us spiritually mature. There is no other way! It's the pathway we must follow in order to be transformed into the image of Christ and reach spiritual maturity. Through discipleship, God grants us life, love, joy, peace, healthy minds, healthy relationships, healthy families, and healthy churches. It's our life's calling and the highest purpose to which we can give ourselves.

Howard Hendricks went so far as to claim, "When a person makes a profession of faith and … is never taken through a formal discipleship process, then there's little hope of seeing genuine spiritual transformation."[13]

---

[12] Bill Hull, *The Complete Book of Discipleship: On Being and Making Followers of Christ* (The Navigators Reference Library 1, 2014, NavPress, Kindle Edition), Kindle Locations 436-437.

[13] C. S. Lewis Institute, *Sparking a Discipleship Movement in America and Beyond*, cslewisinstitute.org, http://www.cslewisinstitute.org/webfm_send/210, Accessed 08/19/2015.

Chapter 9: What to Do After Salvation?

To the degree we are committed to discipleship will be the degree to which we attain spiritual maturity. To the degree we neglect our commitment to discipleship will be the degree to which we suffer destruction, devastation, and eternal loss.

Make a Commitment to Grow in Christ Through Discipleship

A proper understanding of discipleship begins with a proper understanding of salvation. If the true essence of salvation is misunderstood, then the importance and role of discipleship will be misunderstood as well. Many contributing factors are affecting the neglect of discipleship, but one of the most significant seems to be the misunderstanding of the relationship between salvation and discipleship.

Our actions and lifestyles are built upon our belief systems; therefore, if we have a faulty belief system, our actions will naturally follow.

Is Discipleship Optional?

Today, many Christians view discipleship as optional. Even though it was the central focus of Christ's and the apostles' ministries, things have changed over the years. What does Christ teach about salvation and discipleship? Is the belief in salvation without discipleship biblical?

Dallas Willard claims that today Christianity as a

whole tends to believe salvation is good enough to get us to heaven, and discipleship is optional.[14] Willard elaborates on the state of Christianity today when he says, "For at least several decades the churches of the Western world have not made discipleship a condition of being a Christian. One is not required to be, or to intend to be, a disciple in order to become a Christian, and one may remain a Christian without any signs of progress toward or in discipleship."[15] In addition, John MacArthur believes that the contemporary teaching that separates discipleship from salvation springs from ideas foreign to Scripture.[16]

The Calls of Christ to "Follow Me" Combine Salvation and Discipleship into One Act

In the accounts where Christ uses the term *follow Me*, they include both a salvation and discipleship call. While some would like to separate Christ's call to salvation from His call to discipleship, they seem to be one and the same, according to Jesus. In other words, salvation and being a disciple go hand in hand. Notice how Christ combines salvation and discipleship together:

Mark 8:34–37: *And calling the crowd to him with his*

---

[14] Dallas Willard, *The Great Omission* (HarperCollins. Kindle Edition, 2009-10-13), p. 4.
[15] Ibid., p. 4.
[16] John MacArthur, *The Gospel According to Jesus* (Grand Rapids, Michigan, Zondervan Publishing House, 1988), p. 196.

Chapter 9: What to Do After Salvation?

disciples, he said to them, *"If anyone would come after me, let him deny himself and take up his cross and follow me. For whoever would save his life will lose it, but whoever loses his life for my sake and the gospel's will save it. For what does it profit a man to gain the whole world and **forfeit his soul**? For what can a man give in return for his soul?"*

There are four other parallel passages where Christ makes similar calls to follow Him (Matt. 10:38-39, 16:24-26; Luke 9:23-25; John 12:25-26). In each call, Christ is addressing two groups: (1) the general crowd, and (2) His disciples.

In Mark 8:34-37, Christ makes a sweeping statement to all, *"If **anyone** would come after me, let him deny himself and take up his cross and **follow me**."* These words would be argued by some to be a call to discipleship only. However, in the same call, Christ uses the terms *lose your life* and *lose your soul*.

How would the terms *lose your life* and *lose your soul* relate to discipleship only? Losing your life and losing your soul would only make sense if the terms refer to salvation, for how could a disciple who is obediently following Christ through denying themselves and taking up their cross lose their soul? It seems clear that Christ combines both salvation and discipleship together into one call. He doesn't see two distinct aspects to the Christian life, but one. His call to salvation was a call to discipleship. Therefore, to be a follower of Christ is to be a disciple.

It would appear, then, that it's unlikely that one can be saved without being a disciple. Salvation, according to Jesus, seems to include much more than mental acquiescence to certain truths about God. It involves an active faith that expresses itself in following Christ. Therefore, salvation and discipleship are one and the same. To be saved is to be a disciple. To be a disciple is to be saved. Unlike some who would like to separate salvation from discipleship, in the calls of Christ to follow Him, they were not separated but combined.

A "Two-Tier" Form of Christianity

Bill Hull, who has written one of the most extensive books on discipleship called *The Complete Book of Discipleship: On Being and Making Followers of Christ*, is deeply concerned about the growing number of Christians who believe that discipleship is optional.

Hull asserts that we've established a "two-tier" state of Christianity. The first level is for those who believe in Christ and then "live primarily as they please," and the second level is for "serious followers" who choose the option of being devoted disciples.[17] He claims, "The church culture in the Global North—along with Australia, New Zealand, and South Africa—has largely

---

[17] Bill Hull, *The Complete Book of Discipleship: On Being and Making Followers of Christ* (The Navigators Reference Library 1, 2014, NavPress. Kindle Edition), Kindle Locations 700-703.

Chapter 9: What to Do After Salvation?

accepted the idea of non-discipleship Christianity: people can be Christians without making any effort to submit to and follow Christ."[18]

Hull continues, "The fact that we've developed this two-tier state of Christianity forces us to retrace our theological footsteps back to the actual message we proclaim. We need to ask ourselves, 'What kind of person does non-discipleship Christianity produce?'"[19]

Hull then elaborates on his claim by stating, "This common teaching is that a Christian is someone who by faith accepts Jesus as Savior, receives eternal life, and is safe and secure in the family of God; a disciple is a more serious Christian active in the practice of the spiritual disciplines and engaged in evangelizing and training others. But I must be blunt: I find no biblical evidence for a separation of Christian from disciple."[20]

As a result of the belief in a two-tier form of Christianity, many view discipleship as optional. Hull alleges, "They believe they can be saved without being a disciple because by and large, the modern gospel teaches that faith equals agreement with a set of religious facts. The problem is that believing in Jesus has no meaning if we don't follow Him in discipleship.

---

[18] Ibid., Kindle Locations 700-703.
[19] Ibid., Kindle Locations 700-703.
[20] Ibid., Kindle Locations 572-575.

Believing without discipleship is not believing; it is agreeing to a set of facts about a religious figure."[21]

Hull claims that preaching a gospel that excludes discipleship is a different gospel: "But because we've preached a different gospel, a vast throng of people think they are Christian/saved/born again when they really aren't! We've made the test for salvation doctrinal rather than behavioral, ritualizing it with walking the aisle, praying to receive Christ, or signing a doctrinal statement."[22]

David Platt shares this similar concern by stating, "Churches today are filled with supposed Christians who seem content to have a casual association with Christ while giving nominal adherence to Christianity. Scores of men, women, and children have been told that becoming a follower of Jesus simply involves acknowledging certain facts or saying certain words."[23]

From a biblical perspective, this view can run the risk of promoting a form of conversion that can easily produce false salvation and a lack of discipleship. It can give the appearance that we can be saved and then live our lives as we please. This mentality leads to the conclusion that we can have the desires of the flesh and heaven too — that we don't need to give up much to be

---

[21] Ibid., Kindle Locations 718.
[22] Ibid., Kindle Locations 740-742.
[23] David Platt, *Follow Me* (Carol Stream, Tyndale House Publishers, 2013), p. 3.

saved. It violates the call of Christ to follow Him in discipleship because discipleship is viewed as optional. Consequently, the state of evangelicalism is suffering as a result, and today we have many spiritually immature Christians.

The Problem with Separating the Gospel into Parts

I admire those who separate the gospel into parts to understand it better. However, discipleship has been negatively affected as a result.

Instead of viewing the gospel as a complete process, there's a desire to separate the initial stage of salvation (belief and faith) from its other parts, such as repentance, obedience, and fruit. In so doing, faith and belief are often elevated and clarified, while the expression of salvation, as evidenced by repentance, obedience, and fruit, is overlooked or misunderstood as works. Instead of viewing the gospel in its entirety, it's divided up and dissected.

While careful analysis of each part has its role, we can run the risk of losing sight of the big picture because we're so focused on the details. Therefore, it's important to look at the entirety of the salvation process to understand what it entails, not just one part of it.

The gospel is only the gospel when it functions in its entirety. On the contrary, the gospel is not the gospel if only part of it is believed and practiced.

Is Salvation Without Discipleship Biblical?

How does the belief that we can be saved without being a disciple affect discipleship? If we believe there are two aspects of salvation and that we can choose the salvation aspect but omit the discipleship aspect, then discipleship will be viewed as optional.

I believe being saved and being a disciple are one and the same. It's like a two-sided coin: on one side is faith in Christ, and on the other side is following Christ. The act of following Christ is the biblical expression of genuine salvation.

I believe if we primarily focus on one side of the coin (belief only) and omit the other side of the coin (being a disciple), we can promote a false gospel. Both sides of the coin represent the coin in its entirety. Discipleship is the *following Christ* side of the coin. Naturally, if we omit the *following Christ* side of the coin, we omit discipleship. This is the great danger of the belief in salvation without discipleship.

God's Grace and Human Effort in Discipleship

Another factor contributing to the neglect of discipleship today is the common belief that grace is opposed to human effort in spiritual growth. We talk a lot about God's grace, forgiveness of sin, and our freedom in Christ, but don't talk much about

Chapter 9: What to Do After Salvation?

responsibility, discipline, and perseverance. We focus on God's role in granting us grace but neglect our role in exerting effort.

Is the belief that God's grace is opposed to human effort biblical, or do they work hand in hand? Is it okay to be lazy and casual in our Christian lives because God will love us no matter what, or is this dangerous water to enter? Is it okay to presume upon God's grace and forgiveness, or is this a treacherous road to walk?

I believe God's grace that enables us to grow in Christ, be victorious over sin, and arrive at spiritual maturity is not opposed to effort. Grace is opposed to earning salvation and God's love, but it's not opposed to the human agent's cooperation with God by exercising effort in spiritual growth. We see throughout Scripture that God is not opposed to effort in doing His will.

Hebrews chapter 11 outlines all the great heroes of faith and exhibits how their efforts pleased God. Each expression of their faith was accompanied by effort.

We also see in the Apostle Paul's life how he cooperated with the grace of God by exercising effort:

1 Corinthians 15:10: *But by the grace of God I am what I am, and his **grace toward me was not in vain**. On the contrary, **I worked harder** than any of them, though it was not I, but the grace of God that is with me.*

Paul notes how he worked harder than the rest of the Apostles with the grace of God, yet he credits God for everything. In this verse, we see a wonderful relationship between the grace of God and human effort. They work hand in hand, God granting grace and the human agent working and applying this grace to their life.

The well-known verses of Philippians 2:12-13 also speak of the role of effort in relation to salvation:

Therefore, my beloved, as you have always obeyed, so now, not only as in my presence but much more in my absence, ***work out your own salvation*** *with fear and trembling, for it is God who works in you, both to will and to work for his good pleasure.*

Working out our salvation means working to become spiritually mature, not working to earn it. It means living out and applying God's Word in our lives, not just knowing something and remaining unchanged.

Working out your own salvation with fear and trembling speaks of the seriousness we should take in our pursuit of spiritual maturity.

In these verses, God expects us to exercise our effort for spiritual growth in Christ. Bill Hull states, "Grace, then, is God's continued gift of enabling us to do good works and to give great effort. These are as much a part

Chapter 9: What to Do After Salvation?

of his grace as the act of salvation or conversion."[24]

I believe the Bible teaches that living by faith encompasses two aspects: (1) what God does, and (2) what we do in response to what God does. Scripture clearly teaches that we are saved by grace through faith and not of works (Eph. 2:8-9). It also teaches that we grow in our relationship with Christ by grace as well (2 Pet. 3:18).

Therefore, every aspect of salvation and every aspect of growth in Christ involves God's grace helping us in the process. Without God's grace, we would have no desire to receive Christ or grow in Him. It's all accomplished by God working in us and granting us the desire to do His will.

God clearly fulfills His role in granting us grace to grow in Christ. However, He doesn't do everything for us, though He enables and grants us grace for everything. He expects us to have a role in applying His grace. As mentioned, we are commanded to *"Work out our salvation."* This means we are to exert effort and work with God's enabling grace. God expects us to do our part in working with Him, and if we don't, we'll fail to reach spiritual maturity and remain stunted in our growth in Christ.

---

[24] Bill Hull, *The Complete Book of Discipleship: On Being and Making Followers of Christ* (The Navigators Reference Library 1, 2014, NavPress. Kindle Edition), Kindle Locations 718-720.

It's important to understand the difference between effort exerted to earn salvation and effort exerted as the result of salvation. Effort exerted to earn salvation is what Scripture calls, a *"false gospel."* Effort exerted as the result of salvation is what Scripture calls *"working out our salvation."* Effort, therefore, doesn't earn our salvation but is what God expects of us as we work out our salvation to become spiritually mature.

For those who misunderstand the true meaning of grace, they'll tend to neglect discipleship as they'll see it as opposed to grace. They'll hold a common belief that God's grace means He'll overlook our lack of obedience, remove the consequences of laziness, and hold us unaccountable for how we live our lives and use the talents He gives us.

Abusing God's Grace

Today, we tend to abuse God's grace. There's a lot of talk among Christians about our freedom in Christ and God's grace. For some, this means they can acquire salvation and then live as they wish. They boast about the grace of God and their freedom in Christ. They assume that because of God's grace, He now just winks at spiritual laziness and overlooks sin. This simply is not true.

The biblical definition of freedom and grace is very different from what many think today.

Chapter 9: What to Do After Salvation?

The biblical meaning of freedom is the ability Christ grants us to overcome sin, not the freedom to be engaged in it. It's freedom over sin, not freedom to sin. It's the freedom and power to do what we should, not the freedom to do as we wish.

The biblical meaning of grace can be defined as God's supernatural enablement that helps us live in such a way as to please God— not the grace to disobey and be unaccountable to the consequences of sin. God's grace empowers us to obey; it doesn't grant us the liberty to disobey and escape the consequences.

Presuming upon God's Grace

For those who presume upon God's grace and elevate forgiveness over obedience, they overlook a fatal flaw in the life of King Saul. He consistently presumed upon the grace and forgiveness of God by disobeying and assuming God would just overlook his sin. As a result, God removed him as king over Israel and said these harsh words to him through the Prophet Samuel:

1 Samuel 15:22-23: *And Samuel said, "Has the Lord as great delight in burnt-offerings and sacrifices, as in **obeying** the voice of the Lord? Behold, to **obey** is better than sacrifice, and to listen than the fat of rams. For rebellion is as the sin of divination, and **presumption** is as iniquity and idolatry. Because you have rejected the word of the Lord, he has also rejected you from being king."*

In God's eyes, obedience pleases Him far more than asking forgiveness and presuming upon His grace. For the believer who chooses to live casually in their obedience to God, and disobeys because they are counting on His grace and forgiveness, should take great pause. To presume upon and abuse God's grace and forgiveness is a serious sin in God's eyes.

God's Grace Does Not Remove Sin's Consequences

Many Christians confuse God's grace and forgiveness of sin with the removal of the consequences. They are very different functions. God certainly forgives and removes our sins as far as the east is from the west, but He doesn't necessarily remove the consequences of them.

King David is a stark reminder of how sin affects our lives. After he committed adultery with Bathsheba and murdered her husband, Uriah, his life was never the same. He lost fellowship with God for a time, lost the son he had from his adulterous encounter, lost his moral authority, ceased to speak out against sin in the lives of his family and nation, remained virtually impotent as a spiritual leader, and lost the respect of others. God loved and forgave him, but there were monumental consequences for his sin.

Dietrich Bonhoeffer reveals a weakness he sees in Christianity today that abuses and presumes upon God's grace. It's the belief that Christians can be saved

Chapter 9: What to Do After Salvation?

and then do as they please because they are under grace. He counters this understanding by stating, "The word of cheap grace has been the ruin of more Christians than any commandment of works."[25] Bonhoeffer claims that true salvation will encompass discipleship and works. He warns against the idea that salvation can be attained apart from obedience and summarizes such a view as "cheap grace."[26] John MacArthur echoes this same concern when he says, "Grace does not grant permission to live in the flesh; it supplies power to live in the Spirit."[27]

Conclusion

The role of discipleship in a new believer's life is paramount. It's the vehicle by which they will grow in Christ and mature in their faith. Therefore, we must encourage and strongly emphasize that new believers get involved in discipleship right away. If there is no formal class in your church, you might consider personally discipling the person whom you led to the Lord.

It's also important to realize that discipleship should be a life-long pursuit for all believers. God's purpose for us is that we would become spiritually mature, and

---

[25] Dietrich Bonhoeffer, *The Cost of Discipleship* (SCM Classics, Hymns Ancient and Modern Ltd., Kindle Edition, 2011-08-16), Kindle Locations 770-771.
[26] Ibid., Kindle Locations 770-771.
[27] John MacArthur, *The Gospel According to Jesus* (Grand Rapids, Michigan, Zondervan Publishing House, 1988), p. 31.

discipleship is the vehicle through which we attain this maturity.

However, some Christians today are neglecting discipleship because they believe they can be saved but not follow Christ in obedience. They want to be saved, escape hell, and go to heaven, but they don't want to make Jesus Lord of their lives. They really don't care about attaining spiritual maturity and are content with little or no discipleship. This is a dangerous belief!

Another factor contributing to the lack of discipleship is the belief that exerting human effort is not that important or is opposed to God's grace.

For resources for discipleship, we have written two books on this topic. The first is the main book, and the second is the study guide companion.

- ❖ *Biblical Discipleship: Essential Components for Attaining Spiritual Maturity*
- ❖ *Biblical Discipleship: Essential Components for Attaining Spiritual Maturity ~ 16 Week Study Guide*

Please visit: ToddMichaelFink.com for book info.

Chapter 10

Seven Ways God Speaks to the Unsaved

How Has God Revealed Himself to the Unsaved and What Do They Know About Him?

God is a self-revealing God who has made Himself and certain truths known to every rational person. The Bible outlines four universal truths God has made known to everyone, and three ways He has made Himself known to most people as well. As a result, God declares that everyone is without excuse in their knowledge of certain truths.

What are these universal truths God has made known to each person? I think you'll find that after reading this chapter, you'll be amazingly encouraged and strengthened to share the gospel.

1. God Has Revealed Himself to Everyone Through Creation

God leaves no doubt that He makes known to every person certain truths about Himself so that they are without excuse. Notice the clarity with which God reveals Himself in these verses:

Romans 1:18–21: *For the wrath of God is **revealed from heaven** against all ungodliness and unrighteousness of men who **suppress the truth** in unrighteousness, 19 because that which is **known about God is evident within them; for God made it evident to them**. 20 For since the creation of the world His invisible attributes, His eternal power and divine nature, have been clearly seen, being understood through what has been made, so that they are **without***

Chapter 10: Seven Ways God Reveals Himself

*excuse. 21 For even though **they knew God**, they did not honor Him as God or give thanks, but they became futile in their speculations, and their foolish heart was darkened.*

This passage begins by claiming that God reveals certain truths to all people.

Theologically, we can divide how God has revealed Himself into two categories: (1) General Revelation, and (2) Special Revelation.

General Revelation deals with general truths about God found in creation and embedded in our hearts. We can look around, gaze into the heavens, and see clearly that God exists, is eternal, powerful, omnipresent, all-knowing, and possesses divine attributes. Based on this general revelation, God will hold everyone accountable for how they respond to it.

Special Revelation deals with the details of the knowledge of God as revealed in His written word, the Bible.

God begins Romans 1:18-21 by stating that He reveals the truth about His wrath against ungodliness and unrighteousness for those who suppress this truth. Notice that those who reject this revelation are choosing to suppress it. Suppress means to hold something down, to lower its importance, to hide it, or cover it up. Therefore, everyone knows about God's wrath against sin, and even though they inherently know it, some choose to suppress it.

God continues and states that certain aspects of general revelation are revealed by God Himself: *"Because that which is **known about God is evident within them; for God made it evident to them**."* God, Himself, is the one who directly reveals and makes this knowledge evident to all.

What is one of the clear ways that God makes Himself known to all? Through creation. God has made several of His attributes known through what He has made: *"His **eternal power** and **divine nature**, have been **clearly seen**, being understood through what has been made."* These attributes are not foggy and unclear, but *clearly* seen. There is no uncertainty here. God has made some of His attributes amazingly clear to all, so no one is without this knowledge. They can suppress it, but it's still embedded within them and clearly known.

God then makes a declarative and powerful statement: *"So that they are **without excuse**."* No rational person can claim that they don't know about God and some of His attributes. The only way they would have an excuse is if God failed in revealing these truths to them, and that's not a possibility. God takes it upon Himself to reveal these truths to everyone, and as a result, they are without excuse.

For those who know the truth about God's existence, His wrath against sin, and some of His attributes, but reject this revelation, God tells us what happens in the depths of their hearts: *"For even though **they knew God**, they did not honor Him as God or give thanks, but they became futile in their speculations, and their foolish heart was darkened."*

It's clear that those who reject God know about Him. The problem is not their knowledge of God and His revelation to them about His existence, wrath, and attributes, but that they do not honor Him and choose to reject His revelation to them. As a result, they *"Became futile in their speculations, and their **foolish heart was darkened.**"*

According to God, there is no such thing as an atheist. They just don't exist. They can claim to be an atheist, but they simply are not. Once again, the only way they could be would be if God failed to reveal Himself to them, but we know this is not a possibility. Therefore, there are no true atheists that exist. In the depths of their hearts, they know there is a God and that He is displeased with their sin.

How does this apply to sharing the gospel with the unsaved, and especially those who claim they don't believe in God? You can simply rest assured that they do know about God and are just suppressing this knowledge. Also, you can take them to Romans 1:18-32 to show them that they indeed do know about God. There's nothing like God's word to speak to the heart of the unsaved.

2. God Has Embedded the Knowledge of Right and Wrong in Everyone's Heart

When God created each person, He wove within their DNA the knowledge of Himself and His law of right and wrong:

Romans 2:14–15: *For when Gentiles who **do not have the Law [God's word] do instinctively the things of the Law**, these, not having the Law, **are a law to themselves**, 15 in that they **show the work of the Law written in their hearts**, their conscience bearing witness and their thoughts alternately accusing or else defending them.*

In addition to the revelation to everyone that God exists, He has written a law of right and wrong in every person's heart.

These verses reveal that when a person who does not have the word of God (special revelation), yet does what is right, they instinctively do so because of the law of right and wrong embedded within their heart, for they "***Show the work of the Law written in their hearts.***"

How did they acquire this law written in their hearts? From where did it come? And does every rational person possess this law? God says that He is the one who has written the law of right and wrong in the DNA of every person. Therefore, everyone has this law written in their hearts because God has written and placed it in the depths of each person.

Chapter 10: Seven Ways God Reveals Himself

Now a person can suppress this law and choose to do what's wrong, but that doesn't erase the fact that they know they are doing wrong.

How does this relate to sharing the gospel with the unsaved? We can rest assured that in addition to everyone knowing that God exists, they also know they are sinners. Therefore, because this knowledge is in their hearts, we don't have to work hard to convince them that they are sinful.

Now while it's important to enlighten their understanding that they are sinful by showing them verses from Scripture like the Ten Commandments and so forth, however, as mentioned, they inherently know that they have sinned and that they will incur God's wrath as a result: *"For the **wrath of God is revealed** from heaven against all **ungodliness and unrighteousness** of men who **suppress the truth** in unrighteousness"* (Rom. 1:18).

3. God Has Given Everyone a Conscience

In addition to God revealing Himself through creation, and writing His Law of the knowledge of right and wrong in everyone's heart, He has also given each rational person a conscience.

Romans 2:14–15: *For when Gentiles who do not have the Law do instinctively the things of the Law, these, not having the Law, are a law to themselves, 15 in that they show the work of the Law written in their hearts, **their conscience***

bearing witness and their thoughts alternately accusing or else defending them.

What is our conscience? It's another type of law that God has given us that accuses or defends us, depending on our actions. In some regard, it's God's divine voice in our hearts that speaks to us. Sometimes our conscience will accuse us of something we have done wrong, and at other times it defends us, and we feel good about what we've done.

For example, if we lie or steal, our conscience condemns us, and we know we've done wrong. At other times, if we help someone in need, do a good deed, pray, read our Bibles, please the Lord, and so forth, our conscience tells us, "Great job!" and we, therefore, feel good inside.

When a person rejects God, their conscience raises its voice and condemns them. No matter how they try to justify and excuse themselves, they still have the still small voice inside them that makes them feel guilty and bad.

Now it's true that by repeatedly ignoring our conscience, choosing to do wrong, and rejecting God, our conscience can become what the Bible calls, seared:

1 Timothy 4:1-2: *But the Spirit explicitly says that in later times some will fall away from the faith, paying attention to deceitful spirits and doctrines of demons, 2 by means of the hypocrisy of liars* **seared in their own**

Chapter 10: Seven Ways God Reveals Himself

conscience as with a **branding iron**.

What is a seared conscience, and what does it have to do with a branding iron? In order to understand this term, we need to understand livestock and ranching. Ask any cattle rancher, and they'll tell you immediately what a branding iron does when applied to the hide of a cow. It sears and kills all the nerve endings in the skin by burning them.

When applied to people, a seared conscience is a person who has desensitized their conscience by repeatedly disobeying it and doing wrong. They have the nerve endings of their conscience seared and have lost their feelings for right and wrong.

Now we must be clear; just because their conscience is seared doesn't mean they still don't have one. It still exists, but they just don't listen to it. They have grown accustomed to ignoring and suppressing the voice of their God-given conscience. They have chosen to suppress God, and they are comfortable and set in their path of disobedience and rejection of God, their Creator, who has clearly revealed Himself to them.

A person with a seared conscience is a hard-hearted person. They're like the person in the Parable of the Sower. When the seed of God's word falls on their soil, their heart is so hard they reject it, and Satan comes and snatches it away. People like this need firm warnings and our patience to plant the seed of God's word in their hearts, hoping it will grow and take root.

How does this apply to us as we share the gospel? Once again, regardless of what a person says about their belief in God and right and wrong, they have a conscience that has been given to them by God, which testifies to the fact that they know there is a God and they are sinners.

4. God Convicts Everyone of Sin Through His Spirit

God also reveals and speaks to every person through the Holy Spirit:

John 16:7–11: *But I tell you the truth, it is to your advantage that I [Jesus] go away; for if I do not go away, the Helper [Holy Spirit] will not come to you; but if I go, I will send Him to you. 8 And He, when He comes, will* **convict the world** *concerning* **sin** *and* **righteousness** *and* **judgment***; 9 concerning sin, because they do not believe in Me; 10 and concerning righteousness, because I go to the Father and you no longer see Me; 11 and concerning judgment, because the ruler of this world has been judged.*

In addition to the other ways God has revealed Himself, He is also speaking to everyone in the world in a general sense through the Holy Spirit. God's Spirit does three things in every unsaved person's heart: (1) He convicts them of sin, (2) He convicts them of their lack of righteousness, and (3) He convicts them of judgment due to their sin.

Chapter 10: Seven Ways God Reveals Himself

These convicting works of God in every unsaved person's life coincide with His other workings in their heart to increase and give greater weight to their sin of rejecting Him.

As we see each additional way in which God reveals Himself to every person, we see a case against them mounting stronger and stronger. Each additional revelation and working of God make the unsaved increasingly guilty. God will not stand condemned in any way on judgment day for sending the unsaved to hell. He has spoken in many ways, yet the unsaved have turned their back on Him and set their sinful heart against Him.

One of the purposes God has in revealing Himself in so many ways to the unsaved is so: *"Every mouth may be closed and all the world may become accountable to God"* (Rom. 3:19).

How does the truth that the Holy Spirit is convicting the world of *sin and righteousness and judgment* affect us as we share the gospel with the unsaved? We can be certain that God is convicting them of sin, working in their hearts, and ministering to them as we speak His truth into their lives.

In summary, these four universal truths we've just looked at apply to everyone and are absolutes. They are truths God has revealed to everyone.

5. God Has Revealed Himself to Many Through Scripture

The next three ways God has revealed Himself are not universal like the first four, but would apply to the vast majority of people.

While there are still unreached people groups who have yet to hear the written word of God, the vast majority of the world has heard something about the Bible. With the advancement of technology, mission efforts, and the Internet, most people today have some knowledge of God's word.

God's word is unique, and unlike any written literature in existence. It's living, and no other book is like it. God inhabits His word and speaks through it:

Hebrews 4:12–13: *For the word of God is **living** and **active** and sharper than any two-edged sword, and **piercing** as far as the division of soul and spirit, of both joints and marrow, and able to **judge** the thoughts and intentions of the heart. 13 And there is no creature **hidden** from His sight, but all things are **open** and laid bare to the eyes of Him with whom **we have to do**.*

Several amazing facts stand out in this verse: God's word is living, it's active, it's piercing, and it judges. Moreover, no one will be able to hide from God who has authored His word and to whom we must give an account to in the end.

Chapter 10: Seven Ways God Reveals Himself

Isaiah 55:10–11: *For as the rain and the snow come down from heaven, and do not return there without watering the earth and making it bear and sprout, and furnishing seed to the sower and bread to the eater; 11 so will* **My word** *be which goes forth from My mouth; it will* **not return to Me empty**, *without* **accomplishing what I desire**, *and without* **succeeding in the matter** *for which I sent it.*

God's word is unique because its Author is unique. It's powerful and will accomplish that for which God intended.

It was by God's word that the universe came into existence, and Jesus Christ is also called the "Word." Therefore, God's word is powerful. He inhabits it, and will judge every unsaved person by it.

What About Those Who Don't Know Anything About the Bible?

Now for those who don't know anything about the Bible, how will God judge them on judgment day? I believe Romans 2:14–16 provides the answer: *"For when Gentiles [unsaved] who do not have the Law [don't have the Bible] do instinctively the things of the Law, these, not having the Law, are a law to themselves, 15 in that they show the work of the Law written in their hearts,* **their conscience bearing witness and their thoughts alternately accusing or else defending them**, *16 on the day when, according to my gospel, God will judge the secrets of men through Christ Jesus."*

God will hold those without any knowledge of His word accountable for the light He has given them. What is this light?

1. Their knowledge of Him through creation (Rom. 1:18-21).
2. The law of the knowledge of right and wrong written in their hearts (Rom. 2:14-15).
3. Their conscience given to them by God (Rom. 2:14-15).
4. The work of the Holy Spirit convicting them of sin, lack of righteousness, and judgment to come (John 16:7-11).

I believe how a person responds to God based on the light they are given will depend on how God will judge them. For those who only have the light of general revelation, they will only be judged by that light. For those who have the additional light of special revelation, they will be judged by that light as well, which will be a much stricter standard.

How does the fact that God powerfully uses His word affect us in sharing the gospel? We can have full confidence that as we share Scripture, God is speaking through His word in the heart of the unsaved. He is inhabiting His word and working simultaneously with us as we share Scripture.

For this reason, I strongly suggest using God's word as early as possible in our conversations with the unsaved. We must understand that we could spend hours and hours involved in trying to combat evolution, atheism, unbelief, and so forth. Realize that our human wisdom is no match for the power of God and His word in the heart of the unsaved to convince and convict them of these inherent truths.

When we speak human words, they are just that, human words. However, when we use God's word, along with our words and testimony in sharing the gospel, the impact skyrockets! So, use God's word as soon as possible in answering any questions that might arise from the unsaved, even their denial of God's existence, etc.

6. God Has Revealed Himself Through the Testimony and Existence of the Church

Christ said that He would build His Church, and the gates of hell would not be able to stand against it. The true and living church is something birthed by Christ, sustained by Christ, and used by Christ. It's a living organism that speaks loudly to the world about the existence of God and the genuineness of His true followers.

Read afresh Christ's words about His Church and the power and presence it has in the world:

Matthew 16:13–18: *Now when Jesus came into the district of* **Caesarea Philippi***, He was asking His disciples,* **"Who do people say that the Son of Man is?"** *14 And* *they said, "Some say John the Baptist; and others, Elijah; but still others, Jeremiah, or one of the prophets." 15 He said to them, "But who do you say that I am?" 16 Simon Peter answered, "**You are the Christ, the Son of the living God**." 17 And Jesus said to him, "Blessed are you, Simon Barjona, because flesh and blood did not reveal this to you, but My Father who is in heaven. 18 I also say to you that you are Peter, and upon this rock **I will build My church; and the gates of Hades will not overpower it**."*

The location of Christ's statement happened at a place called Caesarea Philippi. Few other places in Scripture provide so much meaning by understanding the location.

1. Caesarea Philippi was an impressive Greco-Roman city near a huge spring that comes out of a cave and is one of the main sources of the Jordan River.
2. It's about 30 miles (48 km.) north of the Sea of Galilee and is at the foothills of Mount Hermon.
3. It was associated with intense false god worship and evil for many years.
4. Nearby, King Jeroboam set up a golden calf and commanded all the Israelites in this area to worship it.
5. Baal worship took place here during the period of the kings of Israel.
6. Later, under the Greeks, it became the key place of worship to the fertility god, Pan. Pan was a half-

Chapter 10: Seven Ways God Reveals Himself

human, half-goat like creature.

7. Then the Romans incorporated it into a place of false god worship as well.
8. Caesarea Philippi was originally called Panion or Panias, after the Greek god Pan. Later it became known as Banias.
9. Herod the Great's son, Philip, established it as the capital of his territory and named it Caesarea to honor the emperor of Rome. It became a large flourishing Roman city.
10. It was known as Caesarea Philippi to distinguish it from other cities named after Caesar.
11. During the time of Christ, there were five main areas of worship to false gods that took place there.

- Herod the Great built a temple right at the mouth of this huge spring to honor Augustus Caesar.

- A courtyard area to the worship of Pan.
- A temple dedicated to the false god, Zeus.
- An upper Tomb Temple of the Dancing Goats.
- A lower Tomb Temple of the Dancing Goats.

12. It was a worldwide gathering place of worship to numerous false gods.
13. It was literally considered the "Gate of the Underworld" (Hades) by the known world at that time.
14. Children would be thrown alive into the entrance to the cave as a sacrifice to the god of Pan, believing this would appease the gods and bring fertility to their crops.
15. Some even believe that men would mate with goats in the courtyard of Pan and on the Tomb Temples in ritualistic fertility acts believing this would help their crops. They would also have goats mating with goats as well in these areas.
16. It was a sick cesspool of evil and represented the worst Satan, and sinful humanity could offer.
17. The disciples were very uncomfortable coming to this eerie, demonic, dark place, and no good Jew would have even considered coming here.
18. However, Jesus purposefully brought His disciples here to embed within their hearts the imperative truth of who He was, what the mission of His church would be, and the astounding power His church would have over evil through Him.

To properly understand the meaning of this passage, we must understand the big question Christ asked and the purpose for which He asked it.

Chapter 10: Seven Ways God Reveals Himself

The question was about who Christ was, His identity, and His essence.

In contrast to all the false gods being worshiped at this site, Christ established that He was the only true and living God that should be worshiped. Following are key truths that must be understood to understand what Christ intended to communicate to us through this passage.

Caesarea Philippi

Peter's Confession Was a Direct Revelation from God

Matthew 16:17: *And Jesus answered him, "Blessed are you, Simon Bar-Jonah!* **For flesh and blood has not revealed this to you, but my Father who is in heaven."*

Christ Will Build His Church

Matthew 16:18: *And I tell you, you are Peter [petros: small pebble], and on this rock [petra: large massive rock],* **I will build my church***, and the gates of hell shall not prevail against it.*

This passage has had two main interpretations throughout church history. The Roman Catholic Church claims that the rock upon which Christ will build His Church is Peter, upon which they build the papacy. Evangelicals claim that the rock is Christ, based upon Peter's confession.

Evidence that the Rock Is Christ, Not Peter:

- Christ used the word *petros* (small pebble) in describing Peter. He used the word *petra* (large rock) in describing upon whom He would build His Church. Christ certainly wouldn't build His Church upon a pebble.
- Christ didn't say He would build His Church upon Peter because He says, "*Upon this rock.*" He didn't say to Peter, "*Upon you.*"
- Peter had three significant failures in his ministry life: (1) In Matthew 16:23, just shortly after Peter's confession of who Christ was, Christ rebuked Peter

    Courtyard to false gods

    and told him, "*Get behind me, Satan.*" (2) Peter denied Christ shortly before Christ's crucifixion. (3) Paul rebuked Peter in Galatians 2:11, in front of everyone for a serious matter regarding the gospel. Christ certainly wouldn't build His Church upon a frail human.

Chapter 10: Seven Ways God Reveals Himself

- Christ is referred to as the Cornerstone and foundation of the church.
- Peter understood he was not the rock upon which Christ would build His church because he states in 1 Peter 2:4-6:

As you come to him, a living stone rejected by men but in the sight of God chosen and precious, 5 you yourselves like living stones are being built up as a spiritual house, to be a holy priesthood, to offer spiritual sacrifices acceptable to God through Jesus Christ. 6 For it stands in Scripture: "Behold, I am laying in Zion a stone, a cornerstone chosen and precious, and whoever believes in him will not be put to shame."

Court of Pan

The rock upon which the Church is being built is Christ, the Cornerstone.

The Gates of Hell Will Not Prevail Against Christ's Church

Matthew 16:18: *And I tell you, you are Peter, and on this rock, **I will build my church, and the gates of hell shall not prevail against it.***

- Christ purposefully took His disciples to this evil Pagan place to show them that His Church would be so powerful that the gates of hell wouldn't be able to prevail or stand against it.
- Gates were used in the ancient world for defensive purposes. They were used to keep an enemy from entering a certain place.
- This means that the church is on the offense, and the gates of hell will not be able to withstand its entry and power.
- Contrary to what some might believe, the church is not on defense in a stationary mode standing its ground.
- God has designed His Church to be in the world, but not of it. This means we should be involved in influencing the world for Christ, not retreating and hiding from it.
- Christ wants His Church involved in society and reaching every hidden corner of it for Him.

How does the fact that Christ's church exists today affect us as we share the gospel? Its existence is a witness that provides evidence and validity to the essence of the gospel. The church is God's idea and not mankind's. It was born in His heart, birthed by His Spirit, and is lead today by His power.

Now understandably, there are many false churches today. Why is this so? Satan knows the power of the church, so He births false churches through false prophets in an attempt to corrupt the church, contaminate the gospel, and confuse the unsaved.

Satan also desires to damage the testimony of Christ's true church, and unfortunately, he has succeeded. Some churches have a poor testimony and, therefore, damage the witness of Christ's church. This is just a sad reality that happens as a result of sinful leadership and followers who choose to follow their sinful nature instead of the Holy Spirit.

Nonetheless, the true church is powerful and provides a witness to the unsaved that God exists, and His true followers have been changed by His Spirit.

7. God Has Revealed Himself Through Changed Lives

No one can argue rationally against a believer's testimony. The fact that billions of Christians throughout history, and today, have been changed by Christ is overwhelming evidence of the power and truth of Christ. This reality speaks loudly to the unsaved and is another way God has revealed Himself to the world. He lives and manifests Himself through the lives and words of His followers.

Many unsaved people have family members, friends, and acquaintances, who are followers of Christ. These provide the unsaved with a clear testimony of Christ's existence and ability to change lives.

The power of a believer's testimony is probably one of the most overlooked factors in sharing the gospel. The Apostle Paul understood the power of his testimony and shared it on a regular occasion (Acts 9:26-30, Acts 22, Acts 26).

Our testimony is a wonderful way to communicate what God has done in our lives. It's real, it's interesting, and it cannot be argued against by a rational person. It's also one of our most vital tools in relating to the unsaved.

Sometimes, the unsaved have the idea that believers were born the way they are. That they just dropped out of heaven already saved and believing what they believe. Our testimonies place us on the same level as the unsaved and allow them to see we were once just like them.

Therefore, I believe God would desire that every believer be able to share their testimony in both a long and condensed version. They should also be able to relate recent events of answered prayer or things God has done for them. This makes God real and brings Him to life before the non-believer.

Chapter 10: Seven Ways God Reveals Himself

Tips for Sharing Your Testimony

1. Write Out Your Testimony

This could be one of the most important factors in giving a clear, concise, and impactful testimony. After you've written it out, memorize it. This will allow you to be able to give a shorter and longer version of it. You could also write it out in an outline form.

2. Pray

Ask God to speak to the heart of the person with whom you are sharing the gospel.

3. Be Careful of Your Terminology

Try to avoid Christian and ambiguous terms. Sometimes we can use religious words that make sense to us but are like a foreign language to the unsaved.

4. Glorify God and Point to Jesus, Not Yourself

Remember, your testimony is about what Christ has done for you. This should show in your voice, actions, and facial expressions.

5. Share How Christ Has Changed Your Life

Tell of your relationship with Christ. Give a comparison of what you used to be like, and what has changed since the Savior came into your life. It's best to present a clear, coherent story rather than a rambling account of your life. Emphasize the main points and don't get lost in too many details. People will only stay with you so long, so don't drag things way out.

Conclusion

God has revealed Himself to every rational person in four universal ways: (1) through creation (2) by writing His laws of right and wrong in their hearts (3) by giving each person a conscience, and (4) through the Holy Spirit convicting them of sin, lack of righteousness, and judgment to come.

Additionally, He has revealed Himself to the vast majority of people in three ways: (1) through His word (2) through the church, and (3) through the testimonies and changed lives of Christ's followers.

When sharing the gospel, we can take the above truths for granted and don't need to spend endless hours trying to convince someone of something they claim they don't believe in, but in reality, they do because God has revealed it to them and embedded it within their hearts.

While it's okay to use our human wisdom and logic, we need to move as quickly as appropriate to using God's word because that's where the power and conviction reside. God inhabits His word and will use it in the heart of the unsaved to minister and speak to them.

Chapter 11

Four Main Excuses the Unsaved Use Against the Gospel

The following are four main obstacles the unsaved will often bring up when the gospel is shared with them.

1. I Don't Believe in God, or I'm Not Sure He Exists

This obstacle is used commonly by the unsaved. As mentioned earlier, according to God, there is no such thing as an atheist. God has revealed Himself to every rational person, so they are without excuse. This revelation is what we have referred to as "General Revelation" and is how God reveals general truths about Himself to all:

Romans 1:18-21: *For the wrath of God is **revealed from heaven** against all ungodliness and unrighteousness of men who **suppress the truth** in unrighteousness, 19 because that which is **known about God is evident within them; for God made it evident to them**. 20 For since the creation of the world His invisible attributes, His eternal power and divine nature, have been clearly seen, being understood through what has been made, so that they are **without excuse**. 21 For even though **they knew God**, they did not honor Him as God or give thanks, but they became futile in their speculations, and their foolish heart was darkened.*

If someone uses this excuse, it's best to take them to this passage of the Bible and show them that they indeed do know in the depth of their heart that God exists.

You can also use the following verses to show them

Chapter 11: Four Main Excuses Used Against the Gospel

that God has also revealed Himself to them through writing His law of right and wrong in their heart and giving them a conscience:

Romans 2:14–16: *For when Gentiles who **do not have the Law do instinctively the things of the Law**, these, not having the Law, **are a law to themselves**, 15 in that they **show the work of the Law written in their hearts**, their conscience bearing witness and their thoughts alternately accusing or else defending them, 16 on the day when, according to my gospel, God will judge the secrets of men through Christ Jesus.*

2. I Don't Believe in the Bible, or I Think It's Been Changed Over the Years and Isn't Trustworthy

Another excuse the unsaved will use is the truthfulness and trustworthiness of the Bible. Even if they do believe in God, they will often attack the Bible. Following are seven ways to defend the truthfulness of Scripture:

The Dead Sea Scrolls

A great way to defend the Bible is by using the evidence of the Dead Sea Scrolls. Following are some incredible facts about this discovery:

1. In around 1947, Bedouin shepherds were tending their goats and sheep near the ancient settlement of Qumran, close to the Dead Sea in Israel. One of the young shepherds threw a rock into a cave and heard

an echo sound. He and his friends later climbed into the cave and found a collection of large clay jars, seven of which contained leather and papyrus scrolls. An antiquities dealer from Bethlehem bought the scrolls, which later wound up in the possession of numerous scholars who estimated the manuscripts were over 2,000 years old. After news of the discovery was made public, Bedouin treasure hunters and archaeologists discovered tens of thousands of additional scroll fragments from 10 nearby caves.

2. The scrolls were discovered in eleven caves between the years of 1947 and 1956. The manuscripts are numbered according to the caves in which they were found.

3. There are around 972 manuscripts that have been found to date. The longest is 26 feet (8 m.) long.

4. They include fragments from every book of the Old Testament except for the Book of Esther (Esther might have been lost or decomposed due to time or may have been damaged by the Bedouin shepherds).

5. The writings consist of biblical manuscripts and other religious writings that circulated during the Second Temple era (516 BC to 70 AD). About 230 of the manuscripts are referred to as biblical scrolls. However, many of the manuscripts were fragmented and had to be assembled.

Chapter 11: Four Main Excuses Used Against the Gospel

6. The Isaiah Scroll, found relatively intact, is 1,000 years older than any previously known copy of Isaiah, and the other scrolls are the oldest group of Old Testament manuscripts ever found.

7. Amazingly, the biblical manuscripts are virtually identical to the manuscripts we have today of the Old Testament. This proves God's ability to preserve His word through the ages.

The dead sea scrolls were the same scriptures Christ and the apostles used. This gives validity to their accuracy:

1. Christ gave full validity to the authority and accuracy of Scripture and used every section of it in His teachings. He repeatedly said, *"So that it might be fulfilled," "It is written," "Have you not read?"* and so forth.

2. Christ used the Old Testament to explain His purpose on earth: *"And beginning with Moses and all the Prophets, he explained to them what was said in **all the Scriptures** concerning himself"* (Luke 24:27).

3. In the New Testament, there are 850 quotes or references to the Old Testament.

4. The New Testament is built upon the Old Testament and cannot be fully understood without it.

The Dead Sea Scrolls show that Christ affirmed the

Old Testament as accurate and supernaturally preserved by God. If He could preserve the Old Testament, then He can continue to preserve both the Old and New Testaments as well.

The scrolls also predate the time of Christ, so all the prophecies in the Bible about Christ's first coming were impossible to be fabricated and made up as some critics claim.

Prophecy Proves the Bible Is Inspired

Only God can predict the future, so prophecy assures us God wrote the Bible. No other writings of mankind that attempt to prophesy attain to the perfection of the Bible.

Some writings have mentioned a few vague prophecies, but they have not come to pass or were so general that it's hard to prove that they did.

There are around 200 prophecies that provide details about Christ's first coming to earth, and Christ fulfilled each of these prophecies in such detail that no rational person can deny it. And regarding Christ's second coming, there are about the same number of prophecies as well, many of which we are seeing fulfilled today before our very eyes.

Prophecy is what sets the Bible apart from any other writing. Once again, some have argued that the prophecies in the Bible were written afterward and are, therefore, fabricated. However, the discovery of the Dead Sea Scrolls annihilates this argument as they predate Christ's birth and ministry on earth.

Archaeology Proves the Truthfulness of Scripture

Throughout the land of Israel, along with other areas like the Middle East, Asia, and Europe, archaeological discoveries prove the Bible to be true. Some can claim God's word is not accurate, but to do so, they would have to wipe the archaeological evidence off the face of the earth.

I've traveled extensively to Israel and witnessed the places myself, along with the evidence, where the events of the Bible took place. The Bible is true, and the more archaeological discoveries that are made, the greater the evidence mounts to support this truth.

God Is Able to Supernaturally Preserve His Written Word

If Christ was so passionate about the truthfulness of Scripture and claimed it was the very word of God, then we too can certainly trust God's ability to preserve Scripture. And if God supernaturally preserved the accuracy of the Old Testament, He can certainly do the same for the New Testament as well.

God Declares His Word Is Inspired

2 Timothy 3:16-17: *All Scripture is breathed out by God and profitable for teaching, for reproof, for correction,* and for training in righteousness, 17 that the man of God may be competent, equipped for every good work.

2 Peter 1:19–21: *And we have something **more sure, the prophetic word**, to which you will do well to pay attention as to a lamp shining in a dark place, until the day dawns and the morning star rises in your hearts, 20 knowing this first of all, that **no prophecy of Scripture comes from someone's own interpretation** [human wisdom]. 21 For no prophecy was ever produced by the will of man, but **men spoke from God as they were carried along by the Holy Spirit**.*

Hebrews 4:12–13: *For the word of God is **living** and **active**, **sharper** than any two-edged sword, **piercing** to the division of soul and of spirit, of joints and of marrow, and **discerning** the thoughts and intentions of the heart. 13 And no creature is **hidden** from his sight, but all are naked and exposed to the eyes of him to whom we must **give account**.*

Matthew 4:4: *But he answered, "It is written, **Man shall not live by bread alone**, but by every word that comes from the mouth of God."*

Matthew 5:18: *For truly, I say to you, until heaven and earth pass away, **not an iota, not a dot**, will pass from the Law until all is accomplished.*

Luke 21:33: *Heaven and earth will pass away, but my **words will not pass away**.*

Isaiah 55:10–11: *For as the rain and the snow come down from heaven, and do not return there without watering the*

Chapter 11: Four Main Excuses Used Against the Gospel

earth and making it bear and sprout, and furnishing seed to the sower and bread to the eater; 11 so will **My word** *be which goes forth from My mouth; it will* **not return to Me empty,** *without* **accomplishing what I desire,** *and without* **succeeding in the matter** *for which I sent it.*

It's useful to use the evidence from the Dead Sea Scrolls, the reality of prophecy, and archaeology in sharing the truthfulness of the Bible. These truths provide overwhelming evidence that the Bible is inspired and has been preserved by God.

Another key factor is to show how Jesus gave credibility to the Old Testament and affirmed it to be the very word of God. Therefore, if God could supernaturally preserve the Old Testament, we can be assured the Bible manuscripts we possess today have been preserved and are accurate as well.

But more powerful than the evidence of the Dead Sea Scrolls and archaeology, is the very word of God itself. Therefore, move as quickly as you can into sharing from the Bible itself as to its claims to be accurate and from God.

Has the Bible Been Altered Over the Years as It Was Copied and Translated?

Many people have the idea that the Bible has been copied, recopied, then translated into a certain language and then copied from that language to another one and so on until today. Therefore, as some believe, its meaning and accuracy have been altered and changed over this long process.

However, this is not how it has worked. The versions of the Bible we have today are using manuscripts dating back close to the time of Christ. And we have a surplus of around 24,000 manuscripts in part or whole that we use in translating the modern manuscripts to be certain we have the most accurate versions. So, the Bible has not been altered due to translation after translation as we're using the oldest and best manuscripts dating back close to the time of the originals.

It's true that we don't have the original manuscripts of the Bible. But that shouldn't be alarming as they were so valuable that they wore out due to their great usage. However, many copies of the originals were made and passed on.

What About All the Different Versions and Translations of the Bible?

Today, we have an abundance of translations of the Bible from which to choose. This is not a bad thing, but good. It shows the value of the Bible and the desire to make it as available as possible.

There are slight variations in the manuscripts and versions of the Bible, but these are small and affect no doctrine. The fact that we have such an overwhelming abundance of manuscripts with such slight variations

Chapter 11: Four Main Excuses Used Against the Gospel

among them is nothing short of a miracle. This proves God's supernatural hand in preserving His word over the ages.

Most of the major translations are going back to the original languages of the oldest manuscripts for their source material. So once again, it's not as if one Bible is being copied to another and so forth.

3. What About All the Different Religions Today, How Can Only Christianity Be True?

This is an obstacle used widely and frequently by the unsaved. And in all honesty, it's a fair question and one we need to be prepared to answer. If not, we'll strikeout with our hearers.

Christ claimed that there would arise many false prophets in the last days who would deceive many. As a result, today, there is a myriad of false religions and teachings circulating. This can be confusing to the unsaved, and as mentioned, a topic that will commonly arise in sharing the gospel.

How can we know which religion is true? The answer is found in the authority of Scripture and the identity of Christ.

The first task in talking about other religions is to establish the authority of Scripture. If this is not done, then it's just one person's belief system over another's. After establishing the authority of Scripture, the next task has to do with the identity of Christ.

False religions do not believe Jesus is fully God and possesses complete deity. They reduce Him to someone created, non-eternal, a good man, a good prophet, a great teacher, a small god, and so forth. So, it all comes down to what a religion believes about Jesus.

Jesus claimed to be much more than a good man, a great prophet, teacher, etc. He claimed to be God in the flesh, Eternal Father, Mighty God, God with us, the Son of God, the Great I AM, and the Messiah.

There are three options available regarding who Christ is:

1. He was indeed who He claimed to be, God in the flesh.
2. He was a liar because He claimed to be God in the flesh but wasn't.
3. He was a lunatic who was out of His mind because He believed He was God but wasn't.

If, as all false religions claim, Jesus is not fully God, then according to them, He would have to be the greatest liar that ever existed, or a lunatic who was out of His mind because He claimed to be God in the flesh but wasn't. And if He was a liar and lunatic, then He can't also be a good man, great teacher, prophet, and so forth. It can't be both ways, Christ can't be a liar and a lunatic, and a good person at the same time. Therefore,

Chapter 11: Four Main Excuses Used Against the Gospel

the only viable option is that Christ was indeed who He said He was, God in the flesh who dwelt among us.

Following are a few verses to equip you in defending the deity of Christ:

John 1:1: *In the beginning was the Word, and the Word was with God, and the **Word was God**.*

John 1:14: *And the **Word became flesh, and dwelt among us**, and we beheld His glory, glory as of the only begotten from the Father, full of grace and truth.*

John 5:18: *For this cause, therefore, the Jews were seeking all the more to kill Him, because He not only was breaking the Sabbath, but also was calling God His own Father, **making Himself equal with God**.*

John 8:58: *Jesus said to them, "Truly, truly, I say to you, before Abraham was born, **I AM**."*

This proclamation of Christ is a quote from Exodus 3:14:

*And God said to Moses, "**I AM WHO I AM**"; and He said, Thus, you shall say to the sons of Israel, "**I AM** has sent me to you."*

This statement was so offensive to the religious leaders that they picked up stones in an attempt to kill Jesus:

John 10:30–33: *"**I and the Father are one**." 31 The Jews took up stones again to stone Him. 32 Jesus answered them, "I showed you many good works from the Father; for* which of them are you stoning Me?" 33 The Jews answered Him, "For a good work we do not stone You, but for blasphemy; and because **You, being a man, make Yourself out to be God."**

John 20:28: *Thomas answered and said to Him, "**My Lord and my God!**"*

Colossians 2:9: *For in Him all the **fullness of Deity dwells in bodily form.***

Philippians 2:9–11: *Therefore also God highly exalted Him, and bestowed on Him the name which is above every name, 10 that at the name of Jesus every knee should bow, of those who are in heaven, and on earth, and under the earth, 11 and that every tongue should confess that **Jesus Christ is Lord**, to the glory of God the Father.*

Hebrews 1:8: *But of the **Son He says**, "**Thy throne, O God**, is forever and ever, and the righteous scepter is the scepter of His kingdom."* This is a quote from Psalm 45:6.

Isaiah 9:6: *For a **child will be born to us**, a **son will be given to us**; and the government will rest on His shoulders; and His name will be called Wonderful Counselor, **Mighty God**, **Eternal Father**, Prince of Peace.*

Jesus was also prayed to, worshiped, and performed every class of miracle to show He was Lord over every aspect of creation:

- Jesus healed all kinds of sickness.
- Jesus had power over the demons and the demonic world.

- Jesus had power over the weather and calmed the sea.
- Jesus had power over nature – He cursed a fig tree, and it died.
- Jesus had power over animals – He cast demons into a herd of swine, performed miraculous catches of fish, and rode into Jerusalem on an untamed donkey.
- Jesus had power over food – He fed 5,000 and 4,000 people on different occasions.
- Jesus had power over death – He raised several people from the dead and rose from the dead Himself.
- Jesus had authority to forgive sins.

Again, if Jesus is not who He claimed to be, then He would only be a liar or a lunatic and not worthy to pay the penalty and consequences of our sins. This, in turn, would leave everyone unforgiven and lost in their sins.

4. I'm Basically a Good Person and Haven't Done Anything Seriously Wrong

Most with whom we share the gospel will indeed have a valid claim that they are generally a good person. They try to help others, be kind and considerate, and do good deeds when they can. However, this doesn't answer the huge dilemma of the root problem of our sin.

Our greatest sin is separation from God, not having

a relationship with Him, and not loving Him with all our heart, soul, mind, and strength. We need to be born again, reconciled with our Creator, and given a new heart and nature by Him. So, just being a generally good person and not doing horrible sins doesn't solve the problem.

Matthew 22:34–40: *But when the Pharisees heard that Jesus had silenced the Sadducees, they gathered themselves together. 35 One of them, a lawyer, asked Him a question, testing Him, 36 "Teacher, which is the great commandment in the Law?" 37 And He said to him,* **"You shall love the Lord your God with all your heart, and with all your soul, and with all your mind."** *38* **This is the great and foremost commandment.** *39 The second is like it, "You shall love your neighbor as yourself." 40 On these two commandments depend the whole Law and the Prophets.*

If the greatest commandment is to love God with all our being, then the greatest sin is not doing so. This is vitally important to understand. A person's major sin is not murder, adultery, stealing, and so forth. These are all sins, but they don't compare to the severity of rejecting a relationship with God and not loving Him.

Therefore, we must establish with the unsaved that their greatest sin is being separated from God and not loving and serving Him with all their heart. If they don't see the root problem of their sin, we can easily get lost in the debate of determining levels of sin, who is a good or bad person, and so forth.

Chapter 11: Four Main Excuses Used Against the Gospel

When a person with whom I am sharing the gospel tries to defend themselves as a good person, I like to ask them if they are loving God with all their heart, soul, mind, and strength? This question usually changes their perspective of sin drastically.

Conclusion

The unsaved will have many unanswered questions and raise certain obstacles against the gospel. Some will use these questions as an excuse to avoid the reality of the truth with which they're being confronted. We need to be prepared to answer these obstacles and patiently replace their wrong beliefs with the truth:

1 Peter 3:15: *But sanctify Christ as Lord in your hearts, always **being ready to make a defense** to everyone who asks you to give an account for the hope that is in you, yet with gentleness and reverence.*

Chapter 12

How to Start and Maintain a Conversation About the Gospel

Chapter 12: How to Start & Converse About the Gospel

Is Being A Good Example Enough?

Starting a conversation with the unsaved in order to share the gospel can be a challenge. To overcome this, many Christians try to live such godly lives before the unsaved that they will hopefully be asked what's different about them. This, in turn, will open the door for sharing their faith.

This is noble as one of the reasons many Christians do not share their faith is because they don't have good testimonies and are not good examples of Christ. Therefore, they fear they'll be labeled a hypocrite or diminished if they share their faith. For this reason, we must have a good testimony if we have any hope in sharing Christ with those who know us. However, is just being a good example and having a great testimony enough?

Now while it's absolutely critical and certainly biblical that we have solid testimonies, be great examples, and live in such a way that others take notice. However, there's more we are called to do. There will be many times when our unsaved friends and family will never ask us about our faith. Moreover, we are also called to share our faith with strangers and those who don't know us.

For this reason, we need to be prepared and discern how we can initiate a conversation with the unsaved about the gospel.

Being Sensitive to the Needs and Hurts of the Unsaved

Studies reveal that different events and experiences in the lives of the unsaved cause them to be more open to God and the bigger questions of life. If we are discerning and looking for these opportunities, we can use them to share the gospel and show how God can help the unsaved in their struggles. These opportunities are available during the following kinds of circumstances and events:

- Big Life Changes
- Graduations
- Marriage
- Birth of a Child
- Death of Loved Ones
- Career Change
- Location Change
- Crises
- Sickness/Health Issues
- Aging Milestones
- Marriage Problems/Divorce/Separation
- Childrearing Struggles
- Financial Problems
- Family Issues
- Relationship Problems
- Depression Issues
- Guilt/Shame Issues

Chapter 12: How to Start & Converse About the Gospel

Conversation Starter Ideas

Following are some ideas for starting a conversation about the gospel:

- Hi! I'm doing a little questionnaire at the park today, asking people about what they believe. Do you have time to answer a few questions?
- Hi! We are out here sharing the gospel, which means good news. Would you like to hear about it?
- Hi! My friend and I live here in the neighborhood and are doing a little project. We're asking people several questions regarding what they believe about God. Could we ask you a few?
- Hi! My brother and I decided to take on the summer project of sharing the gospel with everyone in our neighborhood. Have you heard about the gospel, which means good news?
- Hi! My sister and I are making an effort to pray for the people and their needs in our neighborhood. Is there anything you would like us to pray about?
- Hello! Here's something (Bible tract) for you to read when you have a chance, or we could talk about it now if you'd like.

Conversation Sustainer Questions

- Do you think people are inherently good or inherently bad?
- How do we know what's right or wrong?
- Do you think there is anything all cultures share that is inherently wrong?
- What do you think happens after death?
- Do you think peace with God is a free gift or something we have to earn?
- Do you have any spiritual beliefs?
- Do you believe in life after death?
- If you died today, do you know where you would go?
- What do you think of "such and such" an issue?

Conversation Tips

- God is with us in our conversations and is working in the heart of the unsaved as we speak.
- Be sensitive about starting "the talk" if you have a limited amount of time.
- Don't force the discussion with the unsaved if they seem resistant. Sharing the gospel works best when they are open and receptive to hearing it. It isn't a failure if you choose to wait for a better

Chapter 12: How to Start & Converse About the Gospel

time.

- Don't feel like you need to push for a decision in the first conversation. If you give them something to ponder and consider, you've done a good job. Change of heart in the unsaved often needs several encounters with the truth (planting, watering, etc.)

Overcome the Awkwardness of Starting a Conversation About the Gospel

Let's face it, starting a conversation and sharing the gospel can be awkward. If we let this stop or hinder us, then we might never share our faith. There is rarely the perfect time to start a conversation about Christ. However, if we want to take advantage of the opportunities God places in our paths to share our faith, we must overcome the awkwardness in doing so.

Try focusing on the eternal ramifications of not sharing the gospel instead of the difficultly or awkwardness of the moment. In God's eyes, your involvement in sharing the gospel is extremely vital:

Romans 10:13–15: *For "Whoever will call on the name of the Lord will be saved." 14 How then will they call on Him in whom they have not believed? How will they believe in Him whom they have not heard? And how will they hear without a preacher? 15 How will they preach unless they are sent? Just as it is written,* **"How beautiful are the feet of those who bring good news of good things!"**

Discern Where to Start the Gospel According to What the Person You're Talking with Believes

The first task in sharing the gospel is establishing the authority of Scripture. If this is not done, then it's just one person's belief system over another's. So, one of our first questions to determine is, "What does this person believe about the Bible?" If they believe in the Bible as the word of God, then we can move on to the next question of whether they believe in heaven and hell. If they believe this, then we can move on to the next question, which deals with what we must do to go to heaven and avoid hell. So, the sequence is as follows:

1. **The authority of Scripture:** This establishes a foundation for all truth. Without it, we are lost in a sea of opinions and personal beliefs.

2. **The reality of heaven and hell:** If heaven and hell do not exist, then the gospel is irrelevant.

3. **What must we do to be saved:** Do all roads and beliefs lead to heaven? Is Jesus the only way to heaven? Is salvation by works or by grace through faith.

This last question is paramount because many false religions might believe in God, the Bible, and heaven and hell, but believe the way to salvation is different than what the Bible teaches.

Chapter 12: How to Start & Converse About the Gospel

The sequence of questions to determine the answers to what our hearers believe about these truths would be:

1. Do you believe the Bible is the inspired word of God and trustworthy?
2. Do you believe in heaven and hell?
3. What do you believe we must do to be right with God and go to heaven?

A great question to determine this last belief is this: "If you were to die tonight and stand before God and He were to ask you, 'Why should I let you into heaven, what would you tell Him.'" The answer to this question will tell you a ton about what the person you're sharing with really believes. It will also tell you upon what they're basing salvation.

Based on the answers to these questions will determine our starting point in sharing the gospel.

Every person with whom the gospel is shared will have a starting point according to what they believe. As mentioned, some people will believe in the Bible, heaven and hell, sin, and so forth. Others might have no idea about these truths and are ignorant or choose not to believe them. Before we know where to begin, we need to know the basic beliefs of our hearers.

What Is the Gospel and How to Share It

The Example of the Apostle Paul

The Apostle Paul provides a beautiful example of how he discerned the starting place from which to share the gospel with his hearers in Athens. Notice how Paul moves from general revelation (what we can know about God through creation) to special revelation (what we can know about God through the Bible) in his talk:

Acts 17:22–31: *So Paul stood in the midst of the Areopagus and said, "Men of Athens, I observe that you are very religious in all respects. 23 For while I was passing through and examining the objects of your worship, I also found an altar with this inscription, 'TO AN UNKNOWN GOD.' Therefore, what you worship in ignorance, this I proclaim to you.* **[Beginning point of general revelation]** *24 The God who made the world and all things in it, since He is Lord of heaven and earth, does not dwell in temples made with hands; 25 nor is He served by human hands, as though He needed anything, since He Himself gives to all people life and breath and all things; 26 and He made from one man every nation of mankind to live on all the face of the earth, having determined their appointed times and the boundaries of their habitation, 27 that they would seek God, if perhaps they might grope for Him and find Him, though He is not far from each one of us; 28 for in Him we live and move and exist, as even some of your own poets have said, 'For we also are His children.' 29 Being then the children of God, we ought not to think that the Divine Nature is like*

Chapter 12: How to Start & Converse About the Gospel

*gold or silver or stone, an image formed by the art and thought of man. 30 Therefore having overlooked the times of ignorance, God is now declaring to men that all people everywhere should repent, [**Beginning point of special revelation**] 31 because He has fixed a day in which He will judge the world in righteousness through a Man whom He has appointed, having furnished proof to all men by raising Him from the dead."*

Paul wonderfully illustrates how he started with general revelation and moved toward special revelation. He took into account the starting place of his listeners and moved them toward Christ and His work on the Cross. We would be wise, as well, to understand what our listeners believe and tailor our beginning point to what they understand and believe about God and salvation.

Conclusion

Overcoming the difficulty in starting and maintaining a conversation about the gospel can be easily achieved by utilizing some of the ideas in this chapter. Try to familiarize yourself with them and memorize a few, so you are prepared when opportunities arise to share your faith.

We must also take into account that every person with whom we share the gospel will have a starting point according to what they believe. We need to learn what a person believes, and then proceed from there.

Chapter 13

What Attitudes Should We Have in Sharing the Gospel?

Chapter 13: What Attitudes to Have in Sharing the Gospel?

Sharing the Gospel Is Spiritual Warfare

Entering into a talk about the gospel with the unsaved is to enter into an arena of spiritual warfare. The battle to win their hearts and minds can sometimes be tense. It's vital we understand the correct attitudes we must have to be effective in our conversations with the unsaved, or we can lose ground to the enemy.

The unsaved don't know it, but they're in the hands of the devil and deceived by him:

2 Corinthians 4:3-4: *And even if our gospel is veiled, it is veiled to those who are perishing, in whose case the **god of this world has blinded the minds** of the unbelieving so that they might **not see the light of the gospel** of the glory of Christ, who is the image of God.*

Whether the unsaved realize it or not, they are blinded by Satan to the gospel, and Satan desires that they stay that way. Our job is to work with the Holy Spirit in removing their blindness by the word of God and His Spirit:

Ephesians 6:12: *For our struggle is not against flesh and blood, but against the **rulers**, against the **powers**, against the **world forces of this darkness**, against the **spiritual forces of wickedness** in the heavenly places.*

We must take into account the reality of spiritual warfare, or we can be naïve, inexperienced, immature, gullible, and ineffective in sharing the gospel.

However, if we understand what's happening behind the scene, we will be more effective in the battle to win the hearts and minds of the unsaved.

Having the Right Attitude Is Paramount

Being engaged in a spiritual conversation with the unsaved can become frustrating, tense, argumentative, and weary. It's easy to become angry and lose the correct attitudes we should have in our conversations.

God clearly tells us what kind of attitudes we should have if we want to effectively share the gospel and rescue sinners out of the grasp of the devil. Therefore, please let the following verses soak in deeply:

2 Timothy 2:24–26: *The Lord's bond-servant must not be **quarrelsome**, but be **kind to all, able to teach, patient** when wronged, 25 with **gentleness correcting** those who are in opposition, if perhaps God may grant them repentance leading to the knowledge of the truth, 26 and they may come to their senses and **escape from the snare of the devil**, having been **held captive** by him to do his will.*

These verses are absolutely vital to apply in sharing the gospel. In fact, I would strongly challenge you to memorize them. I can't tell you how many times I've been engaged in conversations with both believers and non-believers when the Lord has reminded me of these verses. It's so easy to become agitated, irritated, and angry in conversations about spiritual matters. However, we must realize that if we lose our temper or

Chapter 13: What Attitudes to Have in Sharing the Gospel?

become irritated, then we lose the battle. It doesn't matter if we say the right thing, if we say it in the wrong way, then we will be considered wrong. People will only see our anger and be blinded to the truth we are sharing. Satan knows this and will do all he can to cause us to lose our patience so our hearers will be blinded to the truth and convinced we are wrong.

Six Correct Attitudes When Talking About Spiritual Matters

Taking into account 2 Timothy 2:24–26, let's focus on the six biblical attitudes God outlines in these verses:

1. We Must Not Be Quarrelsome

A quarrelsome person is hot-tempered, contentious, irritable, argumentative, hotheaded, snappy, touchy, and dissentious.

Being quarrelsome is also defined as foolish: *"Keeping away from strife is an honor for a man, but any fool will quarrel"* (Prov. 20:3).

A quarrelsome person displays a fighting spirit whose main purpose is to win an argument. It's prideful, childish, and immature. It cares more about winning than convincing.

When talking with the unsaved, our goal is to be loving and patient with them. We're trying to rescue them from the captivity of Satan, and the lies He has convinced them are true. This will only happen through patient teaching and dialogue.

2. We Must Be Kind

Being kind is being warm-hearted, considerate, respectful, tender-hearted, affectionate, thoughtful, compassionate, displaying empathy, sympathy, understanding, and friendly.

If the unsaved, or any person with whom we are talking to about spiritual matters senses that we don't love and are not truly concerned about them, will block out and resist our words. Therefore, being kind will keep them on track with us and allow our words to minister to them.

3. We Must Be Able to Teach

God says that we must also be able to teach. Teaching someone means that we instruct them, guide them, lead them, and replace wrong thoughts and beliefs with correct ones.

In order to teach someone, we must be knowledgeable. We need to know God's word well and understand the general arguments against the Bible, God, and the gospel. We should know and be able to articulate our testimony and be graceful and patient as we teach.

God says that we must be ready and prepared to give an answer to those who we talk to about the gospel:

Chapter 13: What Attitudes to Have in Sharing the Gospel?

1 Peter 3:15: *But sanctify Christ as Lord in your hearts,* ***always being ready to make a defense*** *to everyone who asks you to give an account for the hope that is in you, yet with gentleness and reverence.*

The NASB and NKJV versions of the Bible use the phrase, *"Being ready to make a defense,"* in sharing the gospel. It denotes a person who has thought through things, are ready and prepared, and know how to defend the truth against the lies Satan has convinced the unsaved to embrace.

The ESV version of the Bible gives additional understanding by using the word ***prepared*** instead of ***ready***:

But in your hearts honor Christ the Lord as holy, ***always being prepared to make a defense*** *to anyone who asks you for a reason for the hope that is in you; yet do it with gentleness and respect* (ESV).

God commands us to be ready and prepared to share the gospel and defend the truth. It's like a person who studies for a test and passes it with flying colors. They studied, did their homework, and aced the test. If we're going to be effective in tearing down the false beliefs Satan has filled the minds of our hearers with, we need to be ready and prepared.

4. We Must Be Patient

Patient in this context means calm, forgiving, long-suffering, gentle, composed, persevering, persistent, mild-tempered, forbearing, unruffled, even-tempered, understanding, and tranquil.

This attitude is certainly needed when battling for the hearts and minds of the lost or misguided. Patience is also an expression of true love: *"Love is patient"* (1 Cor. 13:4). When we are patient and hang in there with someone difficult or challenging, we truly show them our love and commitment to rescuing them from the lies with which they and Satan have filled their minds.

5. We Must Be Gentle

Displaying gentleness when sharing the gospel or talking with someone about spiritual matters means we are tender, soft, compassionate, considerate, temperate, and kind-hearted. It's the opposite of rough, hard, violent, harsh, mean, rude, agitated, disagreeable, and irritable.

Gentleness is one of the fruits or attitudes of a person who is filled and controlled by the Holy Spirit:

Galatians 5:22–23: *But the fruit of the Spirit is love, joy, peace, patience, kindness, goodness, faithfulness, 23* ***gentleness****, self-control; against such things there is no law.*

God also links the attitude of gentleness as necessary when sharing the gospel:

1 Peter 3:15: *But sanctify Christ as Lord in your hearts, always being ready to make a defense to everyone who asks*

Chapter 13: What Attitudes to Have in Sharing the Gospel?

you to give an account for the hope that is in you, yet with ***gentleness*** *and reverence."*

6. We Must Be Respectful

Being respectful means we treat others with dignity and civility. We don't belittle them, devalue their thoughts, mock them, ridicule them, or inconsiderate to them when sharing the gospel.

How to Tear Down Fortresses and Strongholds

Our task in sharing the gospel, or talking with others about spiritual matters, is to replace untruth with truth. God uses terms like *fortresses* and *strongholds* as synonymous for wrong beliefs:

2 Corinthians 10:3–5: *For though we walk in the flesh, we do not war according to the flesh, 4 for the weapons of our warfare are not of the flesh, but divinely powerful for the* **destruction of fortresses***. 5 We are destroying* **speculations** *and every* **lofty thing** *raised up* **against the knowledge of God***, and we are taking* **every thought** *captive to the* **obedience** *of Christ.* The ESV Bible uses the term ***stronghold*** instead of *fortress*.

These fortresses or strongholds are systems of beliefs, philosophies, thoughts, and so forth that people believe are true but are not.

Our job is to tear down these fortresses and strongholds by using the word of God with the right attitude. Often, it's hard work and requires patience.

Those who hold to certain beliefs are totally convinced they are right. Most of the time, their wrong beliefs are based on their culture, experiences, beliefs of others, and their own self-thought process and not on the Bible. Therefore, to be effective, we need to know God's word and be able to accurately use it according to each wrong belief or philosophy we face:

2 Timothy 2:15: *Be **diligent** to present yourself approved to God as a workman who does not need to be ashamed, **accurately handling the word of truth**.*

As we share the truth of God's word accurately with those who are bound in wrong beliefs, we slowly tear down their fortresses and strongholds of wrong beliefs and replace them with correct thinking and truth. We must understand what's happening in this process so we can be patient and calm. Engaging in this activity is entering into spiritual warfare as Satan will do all he can to continue to blind the eyes and hearts of those with whom we are sharing.

What About Jesus, Didn't He Become Angry and Violent?

Some might wonder why Jesus became angry on occasion, and even made a whip and cleansed the temple by driving out the moneychangers. Isn't this contrary to what the Scriptures we've been considering teach? The following are some thoughts I believe reconcile this contrast.

Chapter 13: What Attitudes to Have in Sharing the Gospel?

1. Jesus was God and displayed righteous anger and indignation. When we are impatient, irritable, frustrated, rude, disrespectful, and angry with others, we are simply displaying sinful attitudes, not righteous indignation.

2. Cleansing the temple was a fulfillment of prophecy that revealed to the nation of Israel and its leaders that Jesus was the Messiah: *"And He made a scourge of cords, and drove them all out of the temple, with the sheep and the oxen; and He poured out the coins of the money-changers and overturned their tables; 16 and to those who were selling the doves He said, 'Take these things away; stop making My Father's house a place of business.' 17 His disciples remembered that it was written,* **'Zeal for Your house will consume me'***"* (John 2:15-17).

3. There were many things Jesus did as God in the flesh that we, as humans, cannot do, i.e., touch lepers, forgive sins, etc. So just because Jesus drove out the moneychangers doesn't mean we should do the same kind of acts.

4. Jesus directed His strongest language toward the religious leaders, and those who knew the truth, yet rejected it. This also was a fulfillment of prophecy: *"Therefore I speak to them in parables; because while seeing they do not see, and while hearing they do not hear, nor do they understand. 14 In their case the* **prophecy of Isaiah is being fulfilled***, which says, 'You*

will keep on hearing, but will not understand; you will keep on seeing, but will not perceive; 15 For the heart of this people has become dull, with their ears they scarcely hear, and they have closed their eyes'" (Matt. 13:13-15). Christ spoke very differently to humble and receptive people.

5. Vengeance belongs to the Lord, not us. Jesus was in His rightful place to drive out the moneychangers and be angry on occasion because He was God in the flesh. Being God, He had the right to exercise vengeance. We don't have that same right: *"Never take your own revenge, beloved, but leave room for the wrath of God, for it is written, '**Vengeance is Mine**, I will repay,' says the Lord"* (Rom. 12:19).

6. I believe we can be bold and firm, but should not be rude, angry, or irritated in doing so. It's good and noble to have righteous indignation; however, we must exercise it with great care, or it can be misunderstood.

Conclusion

It becomes clear that to be effective in sharing the gospel, we must have godly and correct attitudes. Once again, we can say the right thing, but if we say it with a wrong attitude our message can be blocked by our hearers and all they'll see is our bad attitudes. They won't see the love and truth of God because our wrong attitudes will blind them.

Chapter 14

What God Does When We Share the Gospel

What Is the Gospel and How to Share It

Christ Is with Us When We Share the Gospel

Christ, who is God, and in whom all authority in heaven and on earth resides, is with us when we share the gospel.

When sharing the gospel or talking about spiritual matters, we can often feel like we're just an insignificant person talking. In some regards, this is true; however, when we realize that Christ is present with us in all our conversations, it will revolutionize our thinking:

Matthew 28:18–20: *And Jesus came up and spoke to them, saying, "**All authority** has been given to Me in **heaven and on earth.** 19 **Go therefore** and make disciples of all the nations, baptizing them in the name of the Father and the Son and the Holy Spirit, 20 teaching them to observe all that I commanded you; and lo, **I am with you always, even to the end of the age."***

Christ said that **all authority** has been given to Me. He didn't say 50%, 90%, or even 99.9% of authority has been given to Me. He said 100% of all authority has been given to Me. He could say this because He was God in the flesh, and presently, He is God almighty as well. Therefore, **all authority in heaven and on earth** has been given to Christ.

Not only does Christ have all authority, but He clarifies where He has this authority. It's in heaven and on earth. Is there any other place besides heaven and

Chapter 14: What God Does in the Heart of the Unsaved

earth? So, we're talking about maximum authority in the universe given to Christ. That's a staggering thought!

Christ then ended His Great Commission Mandate with this powerful statement: "*And lo, **I am with you always, even to the end of the age**.*" As a result of this statement, the powerful truth and reality is that the One in whom all authority resides in the universe is with us as we share the gospel.

Therefore, we are not alone. We have the One in whom all power resides in the universe with us, helping us as we share the gospel. Amazing! So, as you share the gospel, understand that Christ is with you, helping you, and working in the heart of the person with whom you are speaking. He also is so passionate about us sharing the gospel that He sovereignly and continually places people in our paths with whom we can share.

God Speaks to the Heart of the Unsaved as We Share His Word with Them

God inhabits His word! For this reason, He says it's living, active, sharp, piercing, and judges the thoughts and intentions of our hearts:

Hebrews 4:12–13: *For the word of God is **living** and **active** and **sharper** than any two-edged sword, and **piercing** as far as the division of soul and spirit, of both joints and marrow, and able to **judge the thoughts and***

intentions of the heart. *13 And there is no creature hidden from His sight, but all things are open and laid bare to the eyes of Him with whom we have to do.*

When we share God's word with others, we can count on God speaking to the heart of the person with whom we are talking. He is inside them, speaking, affirming, convicting, working, and ministering to them.

Therefore, we are in partnership with God. We are speaking His word and truths, and He is inside them speaking as well. For this reason, we are not alone. God is with us and using our words from Scripture to bring a person to salvation and the knowledge of Himself.

What an encouraging truth to understand and embrace. This should give us great boldness and encouragement to share the gospel!

The Role of the Holy Spirit in the Heart of the Unsaved

Not only do we have Christ with us in the evangelism process, and God inhabiting and using His word in the heart of the person with whom we are sharing, but the Holy Spirit is working in them as well:

Matthew 16:7–11: *But I tell you the truth, it is to your advantage that I go away; for if I do not go away, the Helper [Holy Spirit] will not come to you; but if I go, I will send Him to you. 8 And He, when He comes, will* **convict the**

Chapter 14: What God Does in the Heart of the Unsaved

*world concerning **sin** and **righteousness** and **judgment**; 9 concerning **sin**, because they do not believe in Me; 10 and concerning **righteousness**, because I go to the Father and you no longer see Me; 11 and concerning **judgment**, because the ruler of this world has been judged.*

The role of the Holy Spirit is to convict the unsaved of three things: (1) sin, (2) righteousness, and (3) judgment. As we minister to the unsaved through God's word, we can count on the Holy Spirit working as well to use our words to convict of sin, righteousness, and judgment.

We can also be certain that even before we say anything to the unsaved, the Holy Spirit has already been working to convict them of these things.

Presuppositional Apologetics

Apologetics is a branch of Christianity that defends the authority of God's Word, the character of God, and Christianity as a whole, and also uses the Bible as an offensive "weapon" (e.g., like a sword) against all other worldviews and opposition.[28]

The phrase translated "to give a defense" or sometimes "give an answer" in 1 Peter 3:15 comes from the Greek word apologia, which literally means

---

[28] Ken Ham & Bodie Hodge, *What Is Apologetics—and Why Do It?*, Answers in Genesis, https://answersingenesis.org/apologetics/what-is-apologetics-and-why-do-it/, Accessed 02/17/2020

"reasoned defense." It does not mean to apologize, which is a common misconception among some who are not acquainted with this thrust of Christianity. It means to give a logical defense of the Christian faith.[29]

Among the branches of Christian apologetics is a specific type known as Presuppositional Apologetics. It comes from the root word to *presuppose*. Presuppose means that we take for granted certain truths that a person knows. Instead of arguing endlessly in a debate about these issues, we can *suppose* (take for granted) that they already know these facts inherently.

For example, in chapter 10, we saw how God has revealed Himself to every rational person and has embedded within them certain truths they know inherently.

These embedded truths are:

1. The Existence of God: Romans 1:18–21

God has revealed His existence to each person, so everyone is without excuse. Therefore, the truth is that there is no such thing as an atheist, and we can show this through God's word.

---

[29] Ibid., Accessed 02/17/2020

Chapter 14: What God Does in the Heart of the Unsaved

2. The Knowledge of Right and Wrong: Romans 2:14-16

God has written His law of right and wrong in every person's heart, so they have this knowledge embedded within them. Therefore, it's not necessary to argue endlessly about this truth because every rational person instinctively knows that they have done wrong and are sinful.

3. Every Person Has a Conscience that Convicts Them of Right and Wrong: Romans 2:15

Along with the inherent knowledge of God's existence, and right and wrong, every rational person has a conscience that speaks to them and convicts them of sin. This is something embedded within them. So, again, we don't need to argue tirelessly about this because they already know this in the depths of their heart.

4. Every Person Is Convicted by the Holy Spirit: Matthew 16:7-8

Everyone receives a sense of conviction by the Holy Spirit regarding their sin, lack of righteousness, and the judgment that awaits them as a result. Therefore, when sharing the gospel with the unsaved, we can be certain the Holy Spirit has already convicted them that they are sinful, and judgment awaits them.

Conclusion

We have Christ, in whom all power resides in the universe, helping us as we share the gospel. Therefore, we are not alone and can count on Christ's grace and help as we evangelize.

Because we can be certain that God is working in the heart of every unsaved person, and has revealed certain truths to them, we don't need to get lost in debating these facts. We can simply point them to God's word and show them what it says. As we do, we can kindly tell them that while they might say they are an atheist or don't believe they are a sinner, in the depths of their heart, they know otherwise.

Presuppositional Apologetics is so alleviating because it removes the burden of endlessly arguing about the existence of God, right and wrong, and the sinfulness of humanity. These truths are embedded in each person, and they inherently know them in the depths of their hearts.

Now while it's appropriate to discuss these matters in some detail, it's not necessary or profitable to get bogged down in them. We can simply show them God's word and move on.

Chapter 15

Are You a Fisherman?

Evangelism is an essential component of the Great Commission Mandate. It's not just for missionaries in a distant land or those with the gift of evangelism, but for all. Everyone should participate in evangelism in some way or another.

Christ's Focus on Evangelism

The Great Commission Mandate includes evangelism:

Matthew 28:19: *Go, therefore, and* **make disciples** *of all nations, baptizing them in the name of the Father and of the Son and of the Holy Spirit.*

Moreover, the corresponding text in Mark 16:15 tells us to: *"****Proclaim the gospel*** *to all creation."*

We also see in the life and work of Christ His concentrated focus on evangelism. He was continually calling people to follow Him, revealing the passion of His heart:

Luke 19:10: *For the Son of Man came to* **seek and to save the lost.**

If we want to be like Jesus, then we should have a passion for evangelism as He does.

We can measure, in part, our spiritual maturity by the level of passion we have for evangelism. If one of Christ's main purposes on earth was to seek and save the lost, it certainly should be one of ours as well, and if not, it reveals we are spiritually immature.

Chapter 15: Are You a Fisherman?

Unfortunately, the majority of Christians don't share their faith or invite their friends to church. For this reason, Christ would sadly say to many Christians today the same thing He said to those during His day:

Matthew 9:37-38: *The harvest is plentiful, but the laborers are few; 38 therefore, pray earnestly to the Lord of the harvest to send out laborers into his harvest.*

Christ Called His Disciples to Be Fishers of Men

Jesus told His disciples that He would make them fishers of men:

Matthew 4:19: *And he said to them, "Follow me, and I will make you fishers of men."*

The same message applies to us today. We are called to be *fishers of men*. A *fisher of men* symbolizes a person who evangelizes. They have a passion for reaching people with the good news of Christ, seeing them saved, reunited with their Maker, and rescued from sin's destructive consequences. It's love in its truest sense.

For the person who neglects evangelism, it should give them great pause. How can they claim to love God and others, and care so little about God's passion for reaching the lost? How can they idly stand by as others destroy their lives, head for hell, and not warn them?

Most Christians Are Not Fishers of Men

In research done by Jon D. Wilke, the statistics regarding Evangelical Christians today who share their faith are troublesome. Wilke reveals, "When it comes to discipleship, churchgoers struggle most with sharing Christ with non-Christians according to a recent study of church-going American Protestants. The study conducted by LifeWay Research found 80% of those who attend church one or more times a month believe they have a personal responsibility to share their faith, yet 61% have not told another person about how to become a Christian in the previous six months."[30] Wilke continues, "The survey also asked how many times they have personally invited an unchurched person to attend a church service or some other program at their church. Nearly half (48%) of church attendees responded, 'zero.'"[31]

Many so-called Evangelical Christians are not only extremely negligent in sharing the gospel, but many don't even invite their unsaved friends to church. Christ said He would make His disciples *fishers of men*. However, for many so-called modern-day disciples, evangelism isn't even on their radar screen.

---

[30] Jon D. Wilke, *Churchgoers Believe in Sharing Faith, Most Never Do*, LifeWay.com, http://www.lifeway.com/article/research-survey-sharing-christ-2012, Accessed 08/04/2015.
[31] Ibid., Accessed 08/04/2015.

Chapter 15: Are You a Fisherman?

Christ Calls Every Believer to Be His Witness

Moments before Christ's ascension to heaven, He repeated the Great Commission Mandate using slightly different words:

Acts 1:8: *But you will receive power when the Holy Spirit has come upon you and you will be **my witnesses in Jerusalem and in all Judea and Samaria, and to the end of the earth**.*

Another term for *witness* is *evangelize*. Christ said some would be witnesses in Jerusalem (their hometown), some would be witnesses in Judea (their county), some would be witnesses in Samaria (their state or country), and some would be witnesses to the ends of the earth (foreign missions). Even though they were to be witnesses in different places, all had the privilege and responsibility to evangelize.

Paul instructed Timothy, who apparently was somewhat shy and timid, to fulfill his responsibility in evangelism:

2 Timothy 4:5: *As for you, always be sober-minded, endure suffering, **do the work of an evangelist**, fulfill your ministry.*

Even though it was uncomfortable for Timothy, he still needed to do the work of an evangelist.

God Has Given All Believers the Ministry of Reconciliation

2 Corinthians 5:18–19: *All this is from God, who through Christ reconciled us to himself and gave us the **ministry of reconciliation**; that is, in Christ God was reconciling the world to himself, not counting their trespasses against them, and entrusting to us the **message of reconciliation**.*

In the same way Christ had, and has today, the ministry of reconciliation (reuniting God with sinners), we have the same ministry as well.

Some feel evangelism is primarily for missionaries or others who have the gift of evangelism. While it's true some might have this gift, it still doesn't alleviate others from participating in evangelism.

We Need to Speak, Not Just Show

A common belief today is that we should let our lives do the talking for us and evangelize primarily by "letting our light shine" before others. Now this belief does contain truth and is what gives us the right to share our faith, yet if we omit the balancing responsibility of evangelizing through speaking, we are misguided.

If letting our light shine was enough, then Christ, being perfect, would have just shown up, not said much, and let His "light shine." However, Christ is

Chapter 15: Are You a Fisherman?

referred to as the "Word" in Scripture who became flesh and dwelt among us (John 1:14).

The spoken word is so important that Christ is called the "Word." And Christ spent His life speaking and doing so much that John ended his Gospel by stating:

John 21:25: *Now there are also many other things that Jesus did. Were every one of them to be written, I suppose that the **world itself could not contain the books** that would be written.*

Virtually every example we see in Scripture where God wants to communicate something, He uses both a clean vessel (letting our light shine) and the spoken word. We need to be careful we don't allow the fear of evangelism scare us away from sharing the gospel through the spoken word, and use the excuse of "letting our light shine" as a reason for not speaking and being bold for Christ.

Ideas for Growing in Evangelism

1. Write out your testimony about how you received Christ.
2. Practice sharing your testimony with loved ones or friends.
3. Share your testimony at church, in a small group, in a Bible study, with a friend, etc.
4. Practice sharing the gospel.
5. Pray for opportunities to share your testimony and

the gospel.

6. Read and study other Bible verses about the gospel.
7. Read books on apologetics (how to defend your faith).
8. Get to know God's word better, so you are not embarrassed when sharing your faith and are more confident (2 Tim. 2:15).
9. Get to know the missionaries of your church.
10. Pray for missionaries.
11. Encourage missionaries by sending them cards, giving them a phone call, etc.
12. Give financially to missionaries.
13. Consider serving as a missionary (either short-term or long-term).
14. Read books on great missionaries and the sacrifices they've made for God.
15. Read books and articles on evangelism.
16. Do a Bible study on evangelism.
17. Look for someone in your church who shares the gospel regularly and effectively, and ask him or her to mentor you in this area.
18. Print Bible tracts provided at the end of chapter 8, and use them in sharing the gospel.

Chapter 15: Are You a Fisherman?

Conclusion

Believers who are not involved in evangelism are believers who don't share Christ's passion for winning the lost. They are failing to obey Christ in fulfilling the Great Commission Mandate and display indifference to the fact that unbelievers are going to hell. If Jesus came to seek and save the lost, then His disciples today should do the same. However, the majority of Christians today are not *fishers of men* as Christ and His disciples were and, instead, seem to loathe evangelism.

There's a huge disconnect today in the lives of many Christians between what they should do and what they do. The fact that the vast majority of Christians don't share their faith or invite their friends to church speaks volumes about their level of spiritual maturity and devotion to Christ.

Chapter 16

What Is Success & Failure in Sharing the Gospel?

Chapter 16: Success & Failure in Sharing the Gospel

How can we measure success and failure in sharing the gospel? The following are some helpful questions to help answer this important question.

Do I Faithfully Share the Gospel?

We can certainly rest assured that if we rarely or never share the gospel, then we have failed. We haven't even gotten off first base. Unfortunately, this is a reality for many Christians. Maybe they have bad testimonies so they feel guilty or hypocritical if they speak, maybe they're just too busy, maybe they don't know how, maybe they're immature and don't know they should, or maybe they just don't care.

Whatever the reason may be, we have failed if we rarely or never share the gospel. Christ gave every believer the command to *"Go into all the world and preach the gospel"* (Mark 16:15). He also said we would be His witnesses in Jerusalem (our hometown), Judea (our county), Samaria (our state or country), and the uttermost parts of the world (Acts 1:8). We are all to be passionate about fulfilling these commands and shouldn't take them lightly.

Do I Faithfully Share All the Steps of the Gospel?

One of the great weaknesses today in sharing the gospel is that many share just part of it. They do well at speaking about God's love and how He desires to give us life, purpose, and eternal life, but neglect or omit the recognition of sin, repentance, and the consequences of rejecting Christ. This means they are sharing an incomplete gospel, which could be classified as a false gospel. As a result, they may cause some to receive Christ for selfish or misunderstood reasons and fall short of genuine salvation.

Do I Faithfully Sow the Seed of God's Word?

One of my favorite parables in the Bible is the Parable of the Sower:

Matthew 13:3–9: *And He spoke many things to them in parables, saying, "Behold, the sower went out to sow; 4 and as he sowed, some seeds fell beside the road, and the birds came and ate them up. 5 Others fell on the rocky places, where they did not have much soil; and immediately they sprang up, because they had no depth of soil. 6 But when the sun had risen, they were scorched; and because they had no root, they withered away. 7 Others fell among the thorns, and the thorns came up and choked them out. 8 And others fell on the good soil and yielded a crop, some a hundredfold, some sixty, and some thirty. 9 He who has ears, let him hear."*

A few verses later, Christ explained the parable:

Matthew 13:18–23: *Hear then the parable of the sower. 19 When anyone hears the word of the kingdom and does not understand it, the evil one comes and snatches away what has been sown in his heart. This is the one on whom seed was sown beside the road. 20 The one on whom seed was sown on*

Chapter 16: Success & Failure in Sharing the Gospel

the rocky places, this is the man who hears the word and immediately receives it with joy; 21 yet he has no firm root in himself, but is only temporary, and when affliction or persecution arises because of the word, immediately he falls away. 22 And the one on whom seed was sown among the thorns, this is the man who hears the word, and the worry of the world and the deceitfulness of wealth choke the word, and it becomes unfruitful. 23 And the one on whom seed was sown on the good soil, this is the man who hears the word and understands it; who indeed bears fruit and brings forth, some a hundredfold, some sixty, and some thirty.

We find in this parable three key players: (1) the sower (2) the seed, and (3) the soils. Nothing changes about the first two players in the story. The sower scatters the same seed on all the soils. The only thing that changes is the receptivity of the soils. Therefore, the response of the soil is what determines if the seed will find a home and grow to maturity.

We are the sowers, the word of God is the seed, and the soil upon which we scatter the seed are people's hearts. We can't determine the response of the soil; the only thing we can do is scatter the seed. When we realize that our job is just to scatter the seed faithfully, then we can rest in God and the outcome. It's the receptivity of the soil that determines the outcome, not us and how wise or gifted we are. Now we do want to be prepared, but once again, we have no control over how the soil will respond to the seed.

If we faithfully scatter the seed, then we have been successful before God in sharing the gospel. If someone rejects Christ and His offer of salvation after we have faithfully shared the gospel using the seed of God's word, then it's not our fault, it's theirs. They have rejected Christ, not us. Therefore, we have been successful and shouldn't feel bad or that we've failed.

Christ shared the gospel with many who rejected Him, and He was a master communicator. So, no matter how great the communicator, if the soil is unreceptive, then the seed just won't penetrate and grow.

Do I Understand that for Some, I'm an Aroma of Life, But for Others, I'm an Aroma of Death?

We are both an aroma of life and an aroma of death. For those who receive the gospel and believe in Christ, we are an aroma of life. However, for those who reject the gospel, we are an aroma of death:

2 Corinthians 2:15–16: *For we are a fragrance of Christ to God among those who are being saved and among those who are perishing; 16 to the one* **an aroma from death to death,** *to the other* **an aroma from life to life.**

For those with open and obedient hearts to the gospel, we are an aroma of life. Through our words God brings salvation to their souls. However, for some, we are an aroma of death. I believe this means that on judgment day when the unsaved stand before God, He

Chapter 16: Success & Failure in Sharing the Gospel

will use our words to add additional weight to His justice in condemning them to hell. Those with whom we shared received the light of the gospel but chose to reject it instead. As a result, we are an aroma of death to them because they chose death over life.

This truth should also encourage us as we share the gospel. God will use our efforts in the lives of both those who receive and reject our words. Therefore, whether those with whom we share the gospel receive it or not, we have fulfilled our responsibility before God. All we can do is share the gospel faithfully, how others respond is between them and God.

How Will They Hear Without a Preacher?

God has chosen to use us in the lives of the unsaved in a vital way. He has called us to an important and beautiful task. For this reason, those who share the gospel are unique and special, and God says their feet are beautiful because they spread good news:

Romans 10:13-15: *For "Whoever will call on the name of the Lord will be saved." 14 How then will they call on Him in whom they have not believed? How will they believe in Him whom they have not heard? And how will they hear without a preacher? 15 How will they preach unless they are sent? Just as it is written,* ***"How beautiful are the feet of those who bring good news of good things!"***

The Workers Are Few

Unfortunately, those who are serious about evangelizing and sharing the gospel are few. This is not God's will, but just a reality that exists. Christ recognized this and said the following:

Matthew 9:35-38: *Jesus was going through all the cities and villages, teaching in their synagogues and proclaiming the* **gospel of the kingdom,** *and healing every kind of disease and every kind of sickness. 36 Seeing the people,* **He felt compassion for them***, because they were distressed and dispirited like sheep without a shepherd. 37 Then He said to His disciples, "The* **harvest is plentiful, but the workers are few.** *38 Therefore beseech the Lord of the harvest to* **send out workers into His harvest.***"*

First, Christ felt compassion for the lost. Do we feel the same? Secondly, Christ saw the lost as those without a shepherd, discouraged, and distressed. Do we see them the same? And lastly, Christ also noticed a big problem. The harvest was plentiful, but the workers were few. That's the same problem that exists today. The problem is not that there is no harvest, it's that we're not looking for it. We're not involved.

Christ then offered up a solution. Pray for more workers. Are we willing to respond to Christ's prayer and be faithful workers in the harvest? I believe God's will is that we would all say "yes" and enter into the harvest field. However, it's up to us. Will we hear His

Chapter 16: Success & Failure in Sharing the Gospel

voice, will we obey it, and will we become workers in the harvest?

Conclusion

The rewards for being involved in the Great Commission Mandate will be beyond understanding. Not only are we being obedient and fulfilling one of our main callings as disciples of Christ, but we will be rewarded in eternity for our labor:

Daniel 12:3: *And those who are wise shall shine like the brightness of the sky above; and those who **turn many to righteousness**, like the stars forever and ever.*

Just think about the reality of the rewards you can have by being serious about sharing the gospel and being involved in the harvest. You will shine like the stars in the brightness of the heavens forever and ever. What a blessing!

Proverbs 11:30: *The fruit of the righteous is a tree of life, and he who is **wise wins souls**.*

Those who win souls are wise because they will save many for all eternity. Think about how grateful those with whom you shared the gospel will be when you're in heaven. You played a role in their eternal salvation. Wow! What a blessing that will be!

James 5:19-20: *My brethren, if any among you strays from the truth and one turns him back, 20 let him know that he who **turns a sinner from the error of his way** will save* *his soul from death and will cover a multitude of sins.*

Those who share the gospel and rescue sinners from the error of their way will cover a multitude of sins. We'll have no way of measuring the heartaches avoided, the suffering, turmoil, and eternal torment erased because of your efforts.

My prayer is that we would become fishers of men and become soul-winners for Christ. He is with us, He uses us, He ministers through us, and He speaks in the hearts of those with whom we talk. Are you in? Will you serve? I'm sure you will. The fact that you've read this book shows you're a person serious about serving Christ.

Some time ago, a short-term missionary participant that served with our ministry said she was around 35 years old before she heard the gospel. Throughout her life, she had many friends who were believers, but they never went out of their way to talk with her about Christ. She now has a passion for sharing Christ and vows she will never be like her Christian friends who remained silent and didn't share with her the greatest news ever given.

Thank you for reading this book, and may God richly bless you, grant you wisdom, and fill you with grace as you share the gospel with the lost and become a master fisherman for Christ. It's all worth it, and the eternal impact immeasurable!

Bibliography

Bonhoeffer, Dietrich. *The Cost of Discipleship.* SCM Classics, Hymns Ancient and Modern Ltd. Kindle Edition. 2011-08-16.

C. S. Lewis Institute. *Sparking a Discipleship Movement in America and Beyond.* cslewisinstitute.org. http://www.cslewisinstitute.org/webfm_send/210.

Gotquestions.org. www.gotquestions.org/definition-sin.html.

Greenwold, Doug. *Being a First-Century Disciple.* 2007. Bible.org. https://bible.org/article/being-first-century-disciple.

Ham, Ken. Hodge, Bodie, *What Is Apologetics – and Why Do It?* Answers in Genesis. https://answersingenesis.org/apologetics/what-is-apologetics-and-why-do-it.

Hull, Bill. *The Complete Book of Discipleship: On Being and Making Followers of Christ.* The Navigators Reference Library 1. 2014. NavPress. Kindle Edition.

MacArthur, John. *The Gospel According to Jesus.* Grand Rapids, Michigan. Zondervan Publishing House. 1988.

Platt, David. *Follow Me.* Carol Stream, Tyndale House Publishers. 2013.

Robinson, Anthony B. *The Renewed Focus on Discipleship: Follow Me.* Christian Century, 124 no 18 S 4 2007, pp. 23-

Bibliography

25. Publication Type: Article. ATLA Religion Database with ATLASerials. Hunter Resource Library.

Tozer, A. W. *I Call It Heresy.* Harrisburg, Penn. Christian Publications. 1974. p. 5. Quoted by Dallas Willard. 2009-10-13. *The Great Omission.* HarperCollins. Kindle Edition.

Wilke, Jon D. *Churchgoers Believe in Sharing Faith, Most Never Do.* LifeWay.com. www.lifeway.com/article/research-survey-sharing-christ-2012.

Willard, Dallas. *The Great Omission.* 2009-10-13. HarperCollins. Kindle Edition.

About the Author

Todd M. Fink is founder and director of Go Missions to Mexico and Holy Land Site Ministries. As a life-long learner, he has earned a Bachelor of Theology Degree, Master of Divinity Degree, Master of Theology Degree, and a Ph.D. Degree in Theology.

He served as a youth/associate pastor for 12 years at an Evangelical church in Oregon (1987-1998).

Todd (Mike) is currently serving as pastor and missionary with Go Missions to Mexico Ministries in Mexico (1998-present) and is also an author, speaker, and teacher. He has a deep passion for God's Word and enjoys helping people understand its eternal truths. He is married to his lovely wife, Letsy Angela, and has four grown children.

Other Books by Todd M. Fink

Israel Biblical Sites Travel Guide

Israel Biblical Sites Bible Companion

Sea of Galilee & Northern Israel Biblical Sites Guide

Jerusalem & Central Israel Biblical Sites Guide

The Negev & Southern Israel Biblical Sites Guide

Biblical Discipleship: Essential Components for Reaching Spiritual Maturity

Biblical Discipleship: Essential Components for Reaching Spiritual Maturity 16 Week Study Guide

Discovering the True Riches of Life

Biblical Analysis of Corrective Church Discipline

Discipulado Bíblico: Principios Esenciales Para Alcanzar La Madurez Espiritual

Discipulado Bíblico: Guía de Estudio: Principios Esenciales Para Alcanzar La Madurez Espiritual

Please visit: ToddMichaelFink.com to see or purchase these books.

Connect with Todd (Mike)

Email: missionstomexico@yahoo.com

Facebook: Todd Mike Fink

Facebook Ministry Page: Go Missions to Mexico

Websites:

- ToddMichaelFink.com
- SelahBookPress.com
- GoMissionsToMexico.com
- HolyLandSite.com
- MinsiteriosCasaDeLuz.com

Notes